"This Is a GREAT BOOK!"

101 events for building enthusiastic readers
inside and outside the classroom
— from chapter books to young adult novels

LARRY SWARTZ

SHELLEY STAGG PETERSON

Pembroke Publishers Limited

To my GREAT nieces and nephews, Matthew,
Zachary, Ayla, Joshua, Max, and Samantha XOX GUL
— Larry Swartz

To Barry Stagg, the best possible companion for
sharing a lifetime of good books
— Shelley Stagg Peterson

© 2015 Pembroke Publishers
538 Hood Road
Markham, Ontario, Canada L3R 3K9
www.pembrokepublishers.com

Distributed in the U.S. by Stenhouse Publishers
480 Congress Street
Portland, ME 04101
www.stenhouse.com

Library and Archives Canada Cataloguing in Publication

Swartz, Larry, author
    "This is a great book!" : 101 events for building enthusiastic readers inside and outside the classroom--from chapter books to young adult novels / Larry Swartz, Shelley Stagg Peterson.

Includes bibliographical references and index.
Issued in print and electronic formats.
ISBN 978-1-55138-308-8 (paperback).--ISBN 978-1-55138-911-0 (pdf)

    1. Reading (Elementary). 2. Fiction--Study and teaching (Elementary). 3. Children--Books and reading. 4. Young adults--Books and reading. I. Peterson, Shelley, author II. Title.

LB1573.S92 2015   372.4   C2015-903649-6
                                        C2015-903650-X

Editor: Kate Revington
Cover Design: John Zehethofer
Typesetting: Jay Tee Graphics Ltd.

Printed and bound in Canada
9 8 7 6 5 4 3 2 1

Contents

1

Novels in the Classroom

"Among the encompassing definitions we could give 'the novel' . . . is this: a novel is a vast heap of sentences, like stones, arranged on a beach of time."
— Jonathan Lethem, *New York Times Review*, 3 June 2007

When young people read a novel, they are invited to step outside their own lives and step along the "vast heap of sentences, like stones," becoming spectators observing imaginary events that might or might not occur in real life. At the same time, they become participants in these events as they are drawn into the story and share the feelings and experiences of the characters. Reading novels thereby provides young people with an opportunity to reflect on human behaviors, emotions, values, relationships, and conflicts. They can discover joy and satisfaction when teachers introduce a selection of books and give them the autonomy to choose their own books for independent leisure reading. When reading novels in the classroom, students do more than learn to read; they create identities as readers and come to feel that they are part of a community of readers.

As young people develop as readers — a lifelong process — they will appreciate a story not only by identifying with the characters but also by seeing through the eyes of the author. In reading and responding to novels, students become aware of how authors use their talents and skills to create stories. They learn to note an author's choices in terms of style, language, action, and characters. As they read, they can rewrite the novel in their minds, creating their own meanings from the novel. They can reflect on their interaction with the text and make connections between that novel and their personal library of literary experiences.

In the classroom, students can explore novels that have been read as a class or by a group, or that the teacher has read aloud. Teachers can introduce and have students engage in response activities that prepare them to read the novel, that accompany the reading of the novel, or that help them reflect on the novel. Novels contain a wealth of stories, and response activities will lead students to uncover dozens more.

In 2015, Daniel Pennac's *Better Than Life* was published in paperback as *The Reader's Bill of Rights*, translated by Sarah Ardizzone, for a young adult audience with illustrations and foreword by Quentin Blake.

Liberating Readers

Sometimes, early enchantment with reading dwindles, diminishes, or even gets quenched as the students move through their school careers. This problem may occur when students are required to read books that do not interest them or are asked to complete novel study activities that they do not find meaningful. It may be that the "study" in novel study does not reflect authentic reading behaviors outside school — how likely is it for an adult reader of *Gone Girl* by Gillian Flynn, for example, to design a new book cover once finished? Talk and the desire to share enthusiasms, criticisms, and wonders about a book can, however, be considered authentic responses. In *Better Than Life*, Parisian author and educator Daniel Pennac challenges teachers to think about ways to sustain or restore students' enchantment with reading with this liberating *Reader's' Bill of Rights*:

1. The right to not read
2. The right to skip pages
3. The right to not finish
4. The right to reread
5. The right to read anything
6. The right to escapism
7. The right to read anywhere
8. The right to browse
9. The right to read out loud
10. The right not to defend your taste

What Is a Great Book?

One Way to Identify a Great Book: The DIRRI Test

In a 9 August 2015 *New York Times* interview, fantasy author Ursula K. LeGuin was asked to name some of her favorite fantasy books. LeGuin, author of the Earthsea trilogy, said that she applies the DIRRI test (Do I ReRead It?) to identify favorite great books. Her list included *Alice in Wonderland*, Gormenghast (series), *The Sword in the Stone*, *The Jungle Book*, and *The Lord of the Rings*.

The underlying premise for this book is that teachers value teaching through great books, as we do. They teach through great books because they believe that reading is a gift that can bring enjoyment. Great books are the best way to help students become independent, purposeful readers who will think carefully about what they have read and develop a lifelong love of reading. A great book can give students vicarious experiences. It can help them live more lives than they think they have, expanding their experiences and worldviews. By doing so, students gain a deeper sense and understanding of their own beliefs, relationships, and values as citizens of the world.

But what *is* a great book? The word *great* has implications we must consider when working with our students. We may be aware of an excellent award-winning book but find it to be outside the realm of our students' lives. Or, a book that we consider to be great may not make it on another critic's list. Yet we can say that there are great books that are popular, great books that are censored, great books for reluctant readers, great books in a continuing series, great books for a lazy afternoon, great books to escort us into night-time sleeps, great books that talk about our communities, cultures, childhoods, and family and friendship circles, great books for our stories, and great books for our dreams. For us, the word *great* denotes a book that will have significant impact on a young reader: that will stay with the reader long after it has been returned to the shelf. The ability to say "This is a great book" depends on the child, the context, the culture, and the occasion.

But we have also asked students what they think a great book is. The statements below come from Junior students at Queen Victoria Public School, Toronto, and their teachers, Ernest Agbuya, Carol Nash, Susan Freypon, and Mehrdad Wellington.

"This Is a Great Book!" — Student Voices

"A great book is like a triple-layered ice cream sundae; it needs to be a combination of ingredients. Some humour, some action, a lot of suspense, maybe something to make you cry when you finish it and maybe just a little bit of romance as a cherry on top. It needs to make you finish reading and then say, 'Damn, that was a good book!' " — M. S.

"There are many qualities to a great novel but I would say three main ones for me are: 1. It's gripping. 2. It has to be moving. 3. It has to make me think." — B. D.

"A book is a good book if YOU make it a good book. If you really like the story, then it is a good story and no one can change that. It does not matter what others think. It is what YOU think is a great book that makes it a great book." — M. K.

"A great book always has to catch the spirit of everyone, no matter how diverse one person may be compared to another. Sure, some people may like a book more than another, but the greatest books have something for everyone. If you only expect one kind of person to read it, you might as well throw in a big 'ages 10 to 11, no exceptions.' " — K. N.

"It's amazing to think that a great book can change your imagination." — M. T.

"A good book becomes a GREAT book when you can pretend to be the character you are reading about and what is happening to the character could happen to you." — S. F.

"I like when the character is a role model." — L. R.

"A great book is when you understand the story and you can't stop reading it. It is a great book when you think of it even at school." — T. A.

"If I can see pictures in my head of what is going on in the book, then it's a great book. If I can relate to the characters or feel what they're feeling, then that's a great book, too!" — S. J.

"Something that makes a book great is the perfect order of the action because it gets you all hyped up." — S. C.

"A great book is not made just for the money. When you put it down, you should be inspired." — K. R.

"A good book is one that is different from others. It should relate to kids but make kids look into something new or make them break away from what they usually see." — I. D.

"A popular question that is discussed is, 'What is the most important part of a book: the setting, plot, characters, theme or conflict?' These are all essential elements to be a good novel, but in order to make a book that everyone will enjoy, conflict is the most important. Now if two authors were on a book tour, and someone asked that question, perhaps the first author would say 'plot' is essential. Then the next author might say, 'No, characters were the most important.' That author would be saying that in a tone that clearly states that he disagrees with the first author. The two authors keep on disagreeing, and by that time, the crowd gets excited about which author is right. This is why conflict is the most essential part to a good book. It gets people excited."— F. F.

Discovering Great Books: Life Lessons

What Did You Learn?

Here are three core questions to ask students so they will consider the impact of reading a novel on their lives:
- What did you learn about reading by reading this book?
- What did you learn about yourself by reading this book?
- What did you learn about life by reading this book?

Readers are bound to have learned something!

"Great books help you understand, and they help you feel understood."
— John Green, author

In *Everything I Need to Know I Learned from a Children's Book*, editor Anita Silvey features recollections from celebrities, authors, sports heroes, and media personalities about life lessons learned from books. From *The Secret Garden*, Katherine Paterson learned a sense of wonder. From *Peter Pan*, Gail Carson Levine learned how precious our term on Earth is. From *Charlotte's Web*, Louis Sachar said he learned that if you see something in writing then it must be true, even if written by a spider on a web. Each writer featured in this anthology shares a favorite novel, picture book, or non-fiction selection to explain how books taught them about inspiration, understanding, principles and precepts, vocation, motivation, or storytelling.

When a book enriches a reader's life or helps a person gain self-knowledge or new understanding of others, it can be considered a great book. Of course, this is not a matter of reading one great book. The more students read, the more they can learn. The more they learn, the more they can grow. If young readers understand that books can inform and teach, and that an author had a reason for writing a book, then they can better consider what makes a book great for them.

Guided instruction, whether it is with a librarian, a teacher, a family member, or a friend, can help young readers of novels to appreciate a book and the experience of reading it. It does not matter whether the book was available from the classroom, school, or community library; purchased from a Book Fair; or given as a gift. As teachers guide students through their reading and response experiences, they are working to enable their students to get the most from the novel. It may be helpful for young readers to have recommendations and thoughtful guiding questions so that they can become better acquainted with great books that may come to matter to them. "When we give children books," Silvey (2009, 11) writes, "we become part of their future, part of their most cherished memories, and part of their lives. Children's books change lives."

A Novel Reader *Despite* School: Recollections by Larry Swartz

Discovering great books was arguably not as easy for me as a child as for a young person today.

Gazing into the rear-view mirror of my own childhood interactions with novels, I have very limited recollection of successful experiences from Grades 4 to 6 in the 1950s and 1960s. There were no Dav Pilkey, Gary Paulsen, or Eric Walters books to choose from. Pickings were slim because it wasn't until the 1960s and 1970s that novels for young people really became a recognized industry in North America.

I was, however, a fellow who enjoyed going to the local library and the bookmobile that came around to our community once a week. Still, most of my reading choices seemed to be biographies and autobiographies. If I signed out fiction, choices were likely drawn from classics, for example, Robert Louis Stevenson's *Treasure Island*.

Then I met *Homer Price*. This book was published before I was born and is likely the one I remember most fondly as a young reader. The book was funny (I thought it was), and there were amusing illustrations that added to the enjoyment of the book. Each chapter was a different episode, so technically the book wasn't a novel but a collection of short stories. Mischief was part of Homer Price's world and where but in fiction could I ever meet a snake oil salesman, encounter a magical chemical called "Ever So Much More So," or battle an unstoppable doughnut-making machine? From Homer (and author Robert McCloskey) I learned about my sense of humor and that I had one.

As for school reading in the middle years, we read *Cue for Treason* by Geoffrey Trease in Grade 7, *The Eagle of the Ninth* by Rosemary Sutcliff in Grade 8, and *The Pearl* by John Steinbeck in Grade 9. I say "we" because everyone in the class read the same novel. Everyone in the class answered the questions, chapter by chapter. The books and the responses we were obliged to prepare did not engage, excite, or entertain me.

I have an ugly memory of completing book reports each year, always with the same format: describe the major characters; describe the minor characters; describe the setting; prepare a plot graph to outline the story events from beginning, rising action, climax, and denouement; and give your opinion of the novel. I dreaded these occasions. The elementary years did not turn me on to becoming a lover of novels, and my passion was ignited *despite* my school literacy experiences, not because of them.

I don't think my journey into the children's book world began until I became a teacher.

I have to thank David Booth who, during my year of teacher training, introduced me to *Nobody's Family Is Going to Change* by Louise Fitzhugh. That book showed how books can help me see families that were different than mine and consider gender issues, as when I read about Emma, who was determined to be a lawyer, and Willie, who wanted to be a dancer.

I also have to thank Olga Stephenson, a teacher-librarian who supported me in my beginning years of teaching. When my father passed away, Olga handed me a copy of Richard Peck's *A Day No Pigs Would Die*. The book helped me deal with my grief. Olga went on to recommend many books to me which, in turn, helped me recommend many books to my students. And my world changed (as did that of the students I taught) with my weekly visits to The Children's Book Store in Toronto and the wise conversations I had with Marion Seary, who really knew what a "great" book was.

From Reading Romp to Purposeful Pursuit: Recollections
by Shelley Stagg Peterson

As for me, I have always loved reading. Although my parents were concerned that I spent far too much time reading when I should have been outside playing, my mother took me to the public library every week to pick up new books when I was a child in elementary school in Edson, Alberta. We reached a happy medium as I became an outdoors reader — finding places on the doorstep, under a tree, even sitting next to the lounging calves in the field when we later moved to a farm to raise cattle.

The public library was one of my favorite places in Edson. I remember that the lower shelf in the children's section housed the series books — that was the first place I looked when left to select books on my own. The librarian knew about the treasures on other shelves, however, and helped me to find more challenging and enriching books than I ever would have found with my head in the bottom shelves. I recognize now that she was introducing me to Newbery Honor and Award books, but at the time, I simply put faith in her and topped up my stack of series books — for example, Nancy Drew, Bobbsey Twins, Pippi Longstocking, and Little House on the Prairie (Laura Ingalls Wilder) — with her suggestions.

I remember reading *Caddie Woodlawn* (Carol Ryrie Brink), *Ginger Pye* (Eleanor Estes), *Roller Skates* (Ruth Sawyer), *Summer of the Swans* (Betsy Byars), and *Strawberry Girl* (Lois Lenski).

The classroom novels I remember were introduced in my Grade 4 health class. My teacher read novels to us on a regular basis. She introduced health curriculum concepts through the lives of characters such as Beezus and Ramona, created by Beverly Cleary, and Billy and his pet owl, Wol, in Farley Mowat's *Owls in the Family*. She integrated literature into a subject area, providing a context for understanding the health curriculum objectives.

The librarian, the most influential person in my reading life, was later replaced by a new friend, Saskia. My family had moved to southern Alberta when I was in junior-high school. Saskia introduced me to Erle Stanley Gardner's Perry Mason books and Agatha Christie mysteries, adding some spicy adult literature to my adolescent reading. I don't remember novels that were read as part of class activities except for high-school English classes, where Ray Bradbury's *Something Wicked This Way Comes* made a big impression on me.

As I look back, apart from the books thoughtfully added to my weekly reading by the wise librarian, it seems that my childhood leisure reading was more of a romp down whatever paths my fancy took me than a purposeful rise up a ladder of what I now recognize as "good" books. Over the years as a classroom teacher and teacher educator, I have caught up on reading classic children's literature, in addition to reading the modern-day novels for children. Yet, when considering how I would advise parents who wish to guide their children's reading lives, I have to say that taking an uneven reading path, with mountains of series and popular culture books, alongside some good books that may have been stumbled upon accidentally or suggested by adults, can still lead to a child becoming a lifelong reader.

FEATURE

Through Wardrobes to New Worlds

by Irene Valentzas

Irene Velentzas contributed this feature when she was a teacher candidate.

Adventure. Independence. Possibility. Magic. These are the things I dreamed of growing up. An unexpected world where I was unexpected: one unburdened by the childhood constraints of dependence — what is what must be, and the dreaded "because I said so." A place of trial and error and reconciliation, of boundary testing, traipsing, and redrawing; a place where I was more than myself, but myself just as I ought to be. These were the sensations fulfilled by the pages of the favorite novels of my youth: ones handed out with bent back covers in the classroom, ones borrowed from best friends, and ones shining and new like candies in their wrappers — each had something to teach me. Growing up, everything I needed to know in life, I learned from my first foray into novels.

Real and Personal Connections

It was under the circumstance of writing a book report that my teacher passed a bin full of books around the classroom one day, instructing us each to choose one. A book report? Wonderful. How to choose? I didn't recognize any of the books in the bin and why take a chance on anything new and risky? I finally selected C. S. Lewis's *The Lion, the Witch, and the Wardrobe*, not for any other reason than the title fascinated me. In what world did these three things connect? In a magical one, I would come to find. So, blindly, I followed Lucy into a stern and stately home with self-interested and avoidant siblings — something I could relate to. I spent a lot of time on my own, but taking that first step through the wardrobe opened a portal for both Lucy and me into a magical world beyond ordinary life.

I felt Lucy's wonder and enchantment at the world and the happiness that comes from opening your heart to peculiar people and possibilities. I found that trusting led to being trusted and being loyal, to loyalty. I found that I could speak up when I felt strongly about something and speak out against someone treating others unjustly. I discovered that I had a voice and that I could use my voice. I began to learn that the world was only what you were determined to make of it — magical or otherwise.

Into Magical Worlds with Friends

Falling through the wardrobe resulted in my falling into many magical worlds, not just that of Narnia. With eagerness I fell into other magical worlds found in books, such as *The Hobbit*'s Middle Earth and *Harry Potter*'s Hogwarts.

In *The Hobbit* I learned that the smallest of people can have the largest of impacts and that sometimes you must abandon caution when called into action. I learned that your self-perception could be redefined if friends told you that you were capable of more than you yourself thought possible. I learned that strangers, when faced with great trials, will band together and become surrogate siblings. I also learned that finding what you want in life may be an epic journey, but that the journey's unexpected detours may alter what you thought you wanted. All the while, I traversed dark dungeons, hazarded great escapes, and flew over mountains. I learned that boldness can be found in unexpected places and that treasure can mean something different to all of us. I learned that wit can outmaneuver even your greatest adversaries. I learned that reading can take you on journeys but no matter how far you go, you can find your way back to where you belong. I learned that accepting the call to action can make you someone you weren't aware you could be.

Growing up, I was excited to go to school, but I didn't always find support from my classmates. Luckily, my foray into these first novels led me to the most fantastical school imaginable, Hogwarts School of Witchcraft and Wizardry — a place where incredible things could be learned and the best adventures happened after dark. The love I found in this book series led me to other readers who enjoyed learning just as much as I did, others who had similarly fallen into a magical world where true friends were forged by loyal bonds and troll conquests. I felt so like Harry, Ron, and Hermione, outcasted, self-conscious, yet determined. I loved that I could see myself in each of them and understand different views through their eyes. Much like Harry, I also came to forge true friendships, based on mutual love of these books, of school, and our desire to be surrogate siblings to one another.

From Reading about Magic to Writing about It

Now, as an adult (or something like it), I still check the back of my closet, just in case, because these books taught me, along with so much else, that life is as magical as you make it. Growing up didn't stop me from trying to make the lives of others magical around me: from turning my first apartment into an enchanted forest for indoor camping, to executing personalized city-wide scavenger hunts; from creating personalized VIP private concert experiences, to creating a midnight mini-putt course in the park. Over time, I learned how to move from dependence to independence through the adventures I had and the lessons I learned along the way.

I still believe in magic and that I am capable of making it, but what I didn't know all those years ago, tumbling from my classroom seat, through the wardrobe, and into Lucy's Narnia, was that these novels would make me not only want to read about magic and make life magical, but inspire me to pursue my own dream of writing. Now,

I write about magical worlds that I can tumble into with the close friends who have inspired me all these years. Because one teacher one time had my class try a different kind of novel study, I found myself, my closest friends, and my lifelong belief in magic. Everything I learned about life, I gleaned from the books I read: I learned about courage, creativity, and compassion, and about how a little imagination goes a long way. I also learned that novels can help us pass through wardrobes to new worlds and that, like Lucy, we can come back home again.

Organizing a Novel Program

Novel Program Components

Students need time . . .
- to hear the teacher read aloud
- to do independent private reading
- to share ideas in small groups
- to respond to their reading
- to celebrate what they have enjoyed

The nature of a novel program may have a great impact on how students embrace the idea of novel reading. A novel program, like any other area of the curriculum, requires long-term planning to determine practices that will need to occur regularly in order to achieve its goals. Decisions need to be made about what kinds of class groupings will best facilitate learning and how to maximize the use of novels you share with the students and have them read. Programs need to evolve to suit the needs and interests of students. The following five components, all based on time, are essential to the development of students as critical and competent readers of literature.

1. Time for the Teacher to Read Aloud

When a teacher reads aloud a novel to the whole class, everyone has the same opportunity to experience the novel format, the author's style, and a good story that happens over time. Listeners can experience a richness of language as they are drawn into the fascination of the story. Good novels, read a section at a time, can connect students to a theme explored over a period of time. Consider, for example, *Hatchet* by Gary Paulsen, which is on the theme of survival. After hearing the story read aloud, students may independently go on to read this novel or other novels by the same author or on the same theme.

Through modeling, teachers demonstrate the importance of reading, a positive attitude towards print, and the satisfaction of enjoying a good story. By choosing novels that students might not select of their own accord, we help students discover other genres, authors, and cultures that they may choose to investigate. Books that are slightly above most students' reading abilities should be considered as appropriate read-aloud material. Read-aloud time is an ideal occasion to broaden the students' world of literature as they are introduced to new authors, the first book in a series, or novels on a particular theme.

TIPS ABOUT READING ALOUD

- Choose a book that *you* are excited or passionate about sharing.
- Let the students in on the choice of the read-aloud. A vote may determine which book will be shared with the whole community. As the novel continues, you are wise to check in to determine whether most students want you to read on.
- Not finishing a read-aloud novel, once started, is acceptable. Sometimes, students' interest wanes. Some students may want to complete the book independently.
- Reading aloud a novel may take several days, even weeks to complete.

- Reading aloud excerpts from a novel can motivate students to choose to read the book in its entirety for their independent leisure reading.
- As noted above, generally, you will want to choose a book that students are unlikely to choose on their own; however, if you introduce an author, a series, or a theme that students may pursue, then the rule can be bent.
- Be sure to use the read-aloud opportunity to demonstrate reading strategies, to promote discussion, and sometimes to invite response activities.
- When reading out loud, share some thoughts or wonderings. In this way, you are further demonstrating what readers do.

APPROACHES TO CHOOSING A READ-ALOUD TITLE

When teachers choose titles to read aloud, a range of motivations is at work. For many teachers, the choice is practical. There may be only a single copy of the novel readily available (e.g., *Wonder*, the popular novel by R. J. Palaccio). Or, a teacher may be so keen on a book that he or she wants to present it for a community read even though students in the class can read the book on their own (e.g., *The Mad Man of Piney Woods* by Christopher Paul Curtis). Then again, the teacher may want to introduce and share a classic. Books such as *Charlotte's Web* by E. B. White, *The Little Prince* by Antoine de Saint-Exupéry, *Mr. Popper's Penguins* by Richard and Florence Atwater, and *The Wind in the Willows* by Kenneth Grahame have been popular read-aloud choices for several generations.

Although we know that most primary teachers read aloud picture books to their classes, students in Grades 3 to 6 are most likely to have novels (or parts of novels) read aloud to them. (For a balanced literacy program, we hope, Grades 7 to 9 teachers would continue the important practice of reading aloud novels or other texts.) As recommendations to be considered, here are some titles that have proven to be successful read-aloud choices for students in Grades 3 to 6:

- *The One and Only Ivan* by Katherine Applegate
- *Tuck Everlasting* by Natalie Babbitt
- *Elijah of Buxton* by Christopher Paul Curtis (Also: *The Madman of Piney Woods*)
- *The Miraculous Journey of Edward Toulane* by Kate DiCamillo (Also: *The Tale of Despereaux, The Magician's Elephant*)
- *Weasel* by Cynthia DeFelice
- *The Iron Man* by Ted Hughes
- *Stone Fox* by John Reynolds Gardiner
- *War Horse* by Michael Morpurgo (Also: *Born to Run, Pinocchio*)
- Hatchet by Gary Paulsen (series)
- *Holes* by Louis Sachar
- *When You Reach Me* by Rebecca Stead
- *Maniac Magee* by Jerry Spinelli
- *Abel's Island* by William Steig

2. Time for Independent Reading

Daily independent reading is an essential part of a novel-based program. To begin, *at least* 15 minutes per day should be devoted to this activity. An extensive selection of readily available novels in the classroom library can contribute to the success of the independent reading program. Students should also be encouraged

In addition to a balanced novel program at school, where there is an independent reading component, the reading that students do outside school is important. See Chapter 3, which discusses how to promote independent leisure reading for each student.

to choose novels from the school or local library, from commercial book clubs, or from their personal collections. To help build their independence, arrange for young readers to witness how others, including you as the teacher, discuss reading interests and habits, choose novels, and share reactions to the books read.

3. Time for Small Groups

Organize groups in response to students' learning needs and re-form the groups often and for reasons beyond the need for direct instruction. Common interests may suggest groups composed of students who can share ideas and feelings growing out of a novel. When grouping students, students' interests should be primary to ensure that the students are committed to completing the books. Teachers may place children in groups according to their reading abilities so that they are discussing books that they can read successfully. In order to ensure successful group discussions, teachers may also group children who are better able to keep a small-group discussion group going with those who have difficulty doing this. If possible, there should be girls and boys in each group. By collaborating on a regular basis in pairs and groups, students can develop the interactive skills necessary to share and build on the foundation of their interests, backgrounds, experiences, and insights.

There are two basic ways to establish group readings of novels:

1. Members of a group read the same novel.
2. Each member of a group reads a different selection by the same author or a book that explores a similar genre or theme.

Five Ways to Organize Groups
- By homogeneous ability
- By heterogeneous ability
- By social skills
- By interests
- By gender

Three Types of Group Management

Once the resources and basic structure for experiencing novels have been established, students need to take control over their learning. Although the teacher's main role at this time is to facilitate, he or she may find that direct instruction, whether one-on-one, in a small group, or with the whole class, can play a significant role in guiding students' reading in preparation for small-group discussions and other response activities. Mini-lessons can be woven into a novel-based program at any time; these may focus on such matters as raising questions about the text, making text-to-self connections, and making inferences about characters' motivations.

1. **Teacher Interactive:** There is direct teacher and student interaction.
2. **Teacher Supervised:** Students progress independently while the teacher guides and monitors progress.
3. **Teacher Independent:** Students read silently and undertake activities; the teacher is not directly involved with the process, but monitors and confers with students about the progress of their reading and independent work.

"Learning to read is a lifelong process. The more time we spend learning to read, the better we become at reading to learn."
— Karen Szymusiak, Franki Sibberson, and Lisa Koch, *Beyond Leveled Books*, page xi

4. Time to Respond

Through response activities, readers come to make sense of what they have read and make links from the world of books to their own life experiences. The variety of forms that readers take to let their voices be heard allows for individual differences in learning styles at the same time that the readers develop critical thinking

"In the Beginning" (page 24) suggests how use of a response line master can invite students to explore a novel, in this case, what the lead sentence of a novel can tell the reader.

skills. Over time, readers in the classroom should vary the ways that they tell others about the novels they have read and share responses through response journals, Literature Circles, and talk, writing, art, and drama activities (see Chapter 4). Graphic organizers are useful tools to help students identify important ideas and consider the relationship between ideas. For example, they might focus on plot structure or relationships among characters.

5. Time for Celebrating

The celebrating time invites students to reflect on their experiences while reading and responding to the novels by sharing artifacts of their responses and promoting books for others to consider reading. When students share their viewpoints with classmates in small- or large-group settings, they have a chance to reveal some of their responses and reactions to story elements as well as to appreciate the viewpoints of others. The process of students recommending books to their peers — promoting and celebrating novels they have enjoyed — needs to be part of the classroom reading community. This component is important because it helps students to reflect upon and enrich their experience of a book. The process of shaping viewpoints into a form, whether verbal, print, drama, illustration, media, or some other artistic form, requires students to think further about the novel and what it means to them. It also requires students to consider how to communicate, persuade, and make ideas understandable to their peers.

In the following sections, we provide specific suggestions for the celebratory activities.

Celebrating an Author through Close Study and Response

An author unit involves the close study of a number of texts written by one author. A collection of a specific author's work is experienced, discussed, and written about. In addition, students learn of the interests, experiences, and styles of the author and can gain an awareness and appreciation of the author as a person.

For a novel investigation of a single author, the teacher may want to read aloud one book as a community read or organize students into groups to read a book by an author using the Literature Circle format (see Chapter 4). If a large number of author titles are available, students might make independent choices among them.

The teacher alone or with the students can

Students can make recommendations of specific novels for others to read and provide short annotated summaries to inform their peers about them.

- make a book display of the author's work in the classroom
- use the Internet to gather information about the author
- display biographical information, articles, posters, and suitable artifacts to help celebrate an author
- collect films, tapes, and YouTube clips of the author's work
- prepare an annotated bibliography of the author's work

Ways to Learn about an Author

1. **Discussion.** Students discuss the author's work, including common patterns or themes it contains; make comparisons to the work of other authors;

consider the author's culture, language, and influences; and share personal responses to several of the novels.

2. **Response through art.** Students create murals, book jackets, posters, sculptures, and mobiles that illustrate the author's work and their response to it. These creations can be put on display.

3. **Response through drama.** Students work in groups of four or five, with each group choosing a favorite scene to dramatize through tableaux, mime, or improvised role-play. They can rehearse and present their drama scenes to one another. If working on a single title by an author, each group can present a different scene from the same novel.

4. **Response through writing.** Students write a letter to the author's publisher in an effort to share their responses, connections, and questions with the author. They can write in their response journals about the author's style. Finally, they can try to re-create the author's style by writing an epilogue to the novel.

5. **Choice of a favorite.** Working in small groups, students present their favorites and discuss why a certain title is their favorite. They might also have an awards ceremony at which books by an author are rated gold, silver, and bronze.

6. **Creation of a historic timeline.** Options encompass preparing a timeline to show publication dates of various novels and listing significant events that students discover about an author (e.g., date of birth, schooling, travels, awards).

7. **An author visit.** Students invite a local author into the class or school to give readings (be aware that a cost is often involved). Before the visit, they familiarize themselves with the author's books, prepare a display, and consider questions to ask their visitor. After the visit, they could write a response, perhaps a letter, sharing what they learned and wonder about, and how they reacted to the information presented by the author. They could also share their responses on a class or school website.

Author Eric Walters can be considered a guru in motivating students to read. For one thing, he has made a vast number of visits to schools. In the feature that follows this author study profile, Walters talks about how he grew from being a teacher to becoming a very popular author.

Writing What He Knows: A Celebration of Author Eric Walters

Author Eric Walters is a children's literature hero. Walters has written more than one hundred books that appeal to young people of different grade levels and interests. His books have been translated into more than a dozen languages and are available throughout the world. Walters has visited hundreds of schools and spoken to more than 1.5 million students throughout Canada to inform students about his writing process and to help motivate young people to read novels.

Before becoming a full-time author, Walters had careers as both a teacher and a social worker. While he was a teacher candidate (in Larry's class) and then a Junior teacher in Mississauga, he wrote his first novel, *Stand Your Ground* (1994). His mandate to write began as an effort to encourage young readers, particularly reluctant readers, to become engaged in literature. He has consistently raised the torch high for connecting young people and books.

Ten YA Novels by Eric Walters

Centered on Sensitive or Social Justice Issues

- *Alexandria of Africa* (classism, poverty)
- *Black and White* (racism)
- *Branded* (sweatshops)
- *Power Play* (sexual abuse)
- *Sketches* (homeless teenagers)
- *Shattered* (Rwandan genocide, homelessness)
- *Special Edward* (learning disabilities)
- *The Taming* (with Teresa Toten) (date abuse)
- *Walking Home* (survival, finding family)
- *Wounded* (post-traumatic stress disorder)

Walters lives by the "write what you know" credo. To become familiar with topics, he does extensive research, mostly firsthand. For example, he played with tigers for the book *Tiger by the Tail*, walked across Kenya for the book *Walking Home*, and climbed Mount Kilimanjaro for the book *Between Heaven and Earth*.

His books expose his readers to a wide range of settings, times, real heroes, and dramatic world events.

- Two important settings are the basketball court (*Boot Camp*) and Africa, a key setting for stories about survival and social justice (*Alexandria of Africa*, *Between Heaven and Earth*, *Walking Home*).
- Settings encompass contemporary (*Stars*, *Catboy*), historical (*The Bully Boys*, *Camp X*), and future time periods (The Rule of Three trilogy).
- Walters pays tribute to Canadian heroes by sharing their stories in novels (e.g., Robert Bartlett in *Trapped in Ice*, Terry Fox in *Run*, Roméo Dallaire in *Shattered*, and Lieutenant James Fitzgibbon in *The Bully Boys*).
- Walters often immerses readers in devastating events ranging from the 1954 Hurricane Hazel (*Safe as Houses*), the tsunami in Thailand (*Wave*), the earthquake in Haiti (*Shaken*), and the fall of the Twin Towers on 11 September 2001 in *We All Fall Down* and *United We Stand*.

His novels have won more than a hundred awards, including the prestigious Children's Africana Book Award and a number of Children's Choice awards. Walters is the only three-time winner of both the Ontario Library Association Silver Birch and Red Maple awards in which more than 250 000 students participate and choose the winner. What's more, he and his wife, Anita, have founded a children's outreach program, the Creation of Hope, which provides direct support, education, and advocacy for more than 500 orphans living in Kikima, a small rural county in Kenya.

The importance of belonging and of an individual's power to make life changes are two overriding book themes. As an author, Walters focuses on creating strong characters who take ownership of their actions. In a 1998 interview for the *Canadian Review of Materials* (University of Manitoba), he said: "One of the societal trends I see is looking for someone to blame for what's gone wrong for you. You've got to take responsibility for things. Rather than finding an excuse to fail, find a reason to succeed." Through his writing and life, Walters has inspired young people to read and to strive to live as engaged, caring citizens.

Passing On a Love of Stories

by Eric Walters

It all started so innocently.

I was the new teacher at a new school. My Grade 5 class of 28 was mainly boys. I quickly found out they were good at three things; gym, lunch, and recess. They didn't like to read. They didn't like to write. They were, however, incredibly good at telling stories — mainly when they were trying to explain to me why they hadn't completed their work or why the vice-principal shouldn't suspend them for some misbehavior.

What I also discovered was that while they were no fans of reading, they were great fans of listening. Each day, often to settle them down, I would read to them. I knew some good books that I thought they might like, but I also consulted with the best resource a classroom teacher can have: the teacher-librarian. She made wonderful suggestions. I read to my class. From *Maniac Magee*, *Owls in the Family*, *Danny the*

Champion of the World to *Frindle*, *Five Days of the Ghost*, and *Hatchet*, I shared this incredible writing with my students. There were wonderful discussions about life — not just the lives and adventures of the characters, but the lives and adventures of my students. After reading one story by an author, they would go to the library to find other stories by the same author they could read themselves. Their writing would begin to take on obvious references to the style of the writer whose work we had just finished. This shared reading became not only their favorite time of the day, but mine as well.

From Teacher to Author

Then two things happened at once: I was starting a unit on local communities and I had to go to a funeral. I was leaving at noon and not coming back that day. We were on the verge of finishing a novel by Martyn Godfrey called *Plan B Is Total Panic*. The time ran out before the pages did, and the lunch bell rang. As had happened more than once, they refused to go for lunch until I finished the story. Which of course I did.

It was a long, emotional service that afternoon. My mind drifted out, and I thought not only of the reaction of my class to that story but to the upcoming unit. I always tried to coordinate a novel to match each unit, whether it was science or social science, but even our wonderful teacher-librarian couldn't think of any novel that was set in our community. Right then, at the funeral, I decided I wanted to write one myself.

Chapter by chapter, I began to write, and share, my novel with my students. To my shock, they were as absorbed in my story as they had been in the amazing novels I'd been sharing. Then again, I had an advantage. This novel, which I called *Stand Your Ground*, was set in their school, Vista Heights. The community was Streetsville. There was a soccer theme because often at the end of the day once they completed all their work, we'd play soccer together. The big water tower beside the school where they'd go for fights was in the book, and in the book the characters went to the tower to have fistfights. What's more, six of the characters in the story were based on students in my class.

Each day when it was time for creative writing, we would write together. They worked on their stories, and I worked on mine. Then, when it was time for shared reading, I read the chapter that I was working on for them. I came to notice that as I worked and risked sharing my writing, they wanted to share their stories with the class. Shared reading became sharing everybody's writing. These kids who didn't want to read or write suddenly wanted to write, read, and share. They saw me not just editing and helping them change their stories but editing and changing my stories. It almost seemed like if I wasn't complaining then neither should they. They got it. And I got it.

At the end of the year, one of my students said to me, "you know, Mr. Walters, your book isn't as bad as most of the garbage in the library" — a high compliment from this group — "why don't you try to have it published?"

I sent the book off to six publishers. Five rejected me, and the sixth accepted. It was amazing! I'd written a book, but still, I wasn't a writer — I was a teacher. At the start of the next year on the first day, the students asked, "What are you going to write about this year?" Apparently, I was a writer. Before finally leaving the classroom to write full time, I'd written more than 25 novels, most of them directly tied to the things I was teaching my students. While writing that first book, we had an author visit from Martyn Godfrey. At break in the staff room I told him about the powerful reaction my class had to his books and casually mentioned I was "writing a book." He was so supportive, positive, and encouraging. Years later, having presented at schools around the world, I am amazed how often teachers tell me they are "writing a book." I try to offer that same encouragement.

Consider these words of poet Muriel Rukeyser: "The world is made of stories not atoms." In this country, with its history of teachers becoming writers, we need to remember that nobody knows and loves stories more than teachers. And nobody is in as good a position as teachers to pass on this love to the children.

Different Approaches to the Novel Program

Research tells us that a majority of novels experienced in middle years' classrooms are through the whole-class community novel: all students read the same book. There are certainly advantages to this method. It is, however, strongly encouraged that during the year, teachers balance their program by facilitating group instruction. Groups can be comprised of half the class each reading a different novel, pairs, or ideally, formations of five or six (see Literature Circles in Chapter 4). To help build community and promote connections among groups (whatever the size), the choice of books can be organized around a focus: a theme, an author, or a genre.

The chart that follows summarizes key ways of organizing the program and points to the value of independent reading as part of a balanced novel program, where each student reads according to personal choices, needs, and interests.

ALTERNATIVE WAYS OF ORGANIZING THE NOVEL PROGRAM

	Strengths	**Challenges**
Whole-class reading of one novel	Minimal organization required Easy-to-manage responses before, during, and after Controllable monitoring and assessing of student progress	Little or minimal student choice Does not address differences in readers' abilities and interests Control of reading experience (e.g., pacing)
Reading in small groups	Requires only a small number of novels in a set Organization of groups by interest or ability Interactive response opportunities	Requires careful management to ensure that all groups are on task Requires students to know how to collaborate in groups Balancing of interaction and instruction with all groups
Independent reading	Greater choice for students Accommodates individual needs and interests Only one copy of a given book required	Need to ensure that all students are reading deeply Management of response activities Monitoring and assessing of the range of reading behaviors and responses

As outlined in the chart on page 19, there are pros and cons associated with each type of instruction. Some teachers choose to balance these types of instruction throughout the year. Reading aloud by the teacher should, however, be ongoing. Beyond using a range of types of instruction, teachers are wise to offer a variety of response modes throughout the year. Advice to beginning teachers on how to create a balanced novel program might encompass the following organization:

Term 1: Whole-Class Community Novel
Term 2: Reading in Small Groups (e.g., Literature Circles)
Term 3: Independent Reading

The next section distills research gathered by 60 teacher candidates who were enrolled in the Literacy course taught by Larry Swartz at the Ontario Institute for Studies in Education, Toronto.

Is Your Classroom an Exciting Book Club?
What a Research Project Reveals

The assignment invited teacher candidates to consider how novels are being taught in Junior and Intermediate classrooms (Grades 4 through 8). Each student was obligated to complete practicum teaching in both the first and second semesters of the Initial Teacher program, and this assignment required them to investigate the planning and implementation of a novel program. In some cases, students were required to teach novels during their practicum and reflecting on the experience would provide data for the assignment. If they were not teaching a novel unit, the following frameworks were offered for this inquiry:

1. Teacher candidates could interview their associate, or host, teacher, preparing questions about the novels used.
2. They could make observations of a novel program they witnessed.
3. They could focus on one student by observing and reflecting on the student's reading and responses. An interview might be involved.

Teacher candidates were asked to consider the following for their research:

- organization of the program: independent, groups, whole class
- timetabling and timeline for the teaching of the novel
- selection of the novels and rationale for the choices
- description of response activities and analysis of the activities
- cross-curricular connections
- assessment of students
- reflections on the strengths and challenges of the novel program
- implications — How might this research inform future practice of teaching novels?

In the final class of the course, students worked in small groups to present their research and discuss their findings. They thereby had an opportunity to make comparisons, consider best practices, and learn about the range of procedures and commitment that teachers have to teaching novels. The data also provided material to confirm or challenge assumptions that I had presented to them in a workshop on novels. Finally, the teacher candidates submitted papers, and I read them carefully to consider the data presented to me and to highlight any emergent themes drawn from the 60 research initiatives.

A Long Way to Go: Overview of Findings

Program Organization
- Fifty percent of the teachers used one novel for the whole class.
- Twenty-five percent of the teachers facilitated small groups.
- Fifteen percent of the teachers introduced an independent reading program.
- Ten teachers chose to read a novel aloud to the whole class.
- Three teachers did not include novels in their Language Arts program.

Response Modes
- Fifty percent of the teachers facilitated Literature Circles. The majority assigned roles through worksheet templates that the students completed.
- Five teachers used reading response journals.
- Five teachers mentioned using the Book in a Box response activity.
- Integrating technology was limited to two or three teachers who discussed iMovie previews and sharing response on wikis.

Book Choices
- Most titles chosen, both for community reads and read-alouds, were from the 20th century. *Tuck Everlasting* by Natalie Babbitt, *Number the Stars* by Lois Lowry, and *To Kill a Mockingbird* were mentioned more than once.
- *The Outsiders* by S. E. Hinton was the title most often mentioned for middle-school years.
- *The Breadwinner* by Deborah Ellis and titles by Eric Walters (*We All Fall Down*, *The Bully Boys*, and *Branded*) represented Canadian authors.
- *Because of Mr. Terupt* by Rob Buyea, *Mr. Stink* by David Walliams, and *Wonder* by R. J. Palacio were the only titles used that were published in the past few years.
- Some Grade 4 teachers relied on Roald Dahl (*James and the Giant Peach*, *The Twits*) to engage the students.

What Is Important: Commentary

Sixty teacher candidates investigated 60 teachers with 60 variations on how to approach novel study. For the most part, it seems that the whole-class community read is still the most common way to teach novels in the classroom. As outlined in the chart (page 19), there are strengths and challenges to this method.

As a children's literature enthusiast, I find it somewhat worrisome that titles released over the past decade are not being considered. Yes, *The Outsiders*, *The Giver*, *Bridge to Terabithia*, and *Hatchet* can continue to engage many young readers. It is hoped that introducing such titles to students will lead them to read more books by the author, in the series, or on a theme. But what are the reasons for such choices? I assume that teachers rely on favorite titles because there are multiple copies of the book in the school, because they have taught these novels for a number of years, and because there are teacher guides available for popular titles — and teacher guides help teachers frame student responses to the books read.

Are the 60 teachers whose approaches to novel study were reviewed representative of the larger picture of novel teaching?

That we don't know for sure; however, I think it's important for teachers to reflect on *why* they are teaching the novels they choose to teach. I think it's important for teachers to stretch their repertoires by finding out about other great books and

Literature Circles have certainly put book talk in the hands of the students. Since some of the student researchers were able to witness Literature Circles in action, they realized that this was a useful instructional strategy that promotes the integration of reading, writing, and talk. Literature Circles are described in detail in Chapter 4.

The "Book in a Box" response activity is outlined on page 102.

implementing strategies that move beyond the traditional question-and-answer format. It's important to give stronger consideration to student choice in reading and response activities. And it's important to consider talk, writing, arts, and technology methods that help students reveal their understandings of a text, have conversations with a text, and talk with one another about books. When a teacher strives to bring these elements into the classroom, it will make that classroom an exciting book club, where enthusiasms can flourish.

Ultimately, this inquiry project was designed to help teacher candidates question and learn about best practices for a reading program that includes novels. Every teacher, novice or experienced, holds assumptions about how literacy should be taught. Engaging in professional development opportunities, taking continuing education courses, reading professional resources, and networking through professional communities in the school help teachers to grow. Researching one's own practice can lead to deeper growth still. The teachers who took part in the research all reflected on what they had learned. *L.S.*

Selected Teacher Candidate Reflections

"Student choice can be difficult to adhere to in terms of resources and practicality, but if we want to encourage a love of reading, we also need to respect the opinions of our students."
— Amanda H.

"What seemed more valuable to me than the assessment I provided of students' participation in Literature Circles, was the students begging to do circles again with another novel."
— Sonia A.

"In my future practice as a teacher, I have learned that there is much potential in teaching through novels. I feel, however, that a program is improved if students are guided into developing deeper meanings and life questions. This can happen by asking better questions."
— Jean Luc X.

"Paying attention to differentiation seems to be a vital theme in education today. I think that the novel program I choose to present in the future certainly can be an important way to address and support the differences that appear in any classroom."
— Kathryn L.

FEATURE

How a Book Chooses a Student

by Anne Porretta

Anne Poretta is a literacy consultant, an avid book collector, and a great baker.

Lamaya's open smile showed her excitement before she spoke. "You know, Mrs. P., while you were reading that chapter aloud, I stepped right inside the covers and stood beside the character. I was invisible, but I could see what he was seeing and feel what he was feeling. It was like I was living his life!"

Lamaya, a new Grade 6 student who had struggled with reading for a long time, got it exactly right. When totally immersed in a novel, we live in the story as it unfolds. Our minds are opened to possibilities and to differing points of view. We stretch, and we grow. Empathy develops, not only with characters with whom we feel a connection, but sometimes even with characters we do not like. Unwittingly, we are transformed.

For those students who read confidently and skillfully, the entry into the book is an easily opened door. But what of the student who struggles, the one who finds the door stuck or locked? For that student, the answer is clear — the teacher is the key.

An Invitation into a Book

In a class of students with diverse reading abilities, there are no easy solutions in matching books to readers. First, we must know our students. What are their needs, their natures, and their lived experiences? What are their interests? With what, and with whom, do they identify? What do they believe about themselves? When we know these things, we can begin to connect our students to texts they can grow in.

The teaching of reading requires a sharing of choice and voice, but initial instructional choice begins with the teacher. I begin the school year with a whole-group novel. It is my role to invite students into the book, much like going on a field trip. What students will get out of it will depend on what they bring to it — their prior knowledge, their ability to connect to content, and their openness to learning new things. The teacher must prepare students for the journey ahead by ensuring that their backpacks are full. We determine what new ideas, concepts, and vocabulary our students will meet in the novel, and we create activities, including artifacts and displays, that promote discussion and new learning before they enter the book.

Engaging students with chosen text is paramount. Author-educators offer teachers a virtual smorgasbord of activities to engage students and deepen their comprehension. Often, drama enactments require preparation but no props. Role play, tableaux, scenarios, debates, and other activities encourage full participation and enjoyment.

Experiencing Novels with Others

In my experience, the whole-group novel study can be a positive and engaging beginning to our work with novels. It sets the stage for new and independent novel work in the months to come. The activities, well practiced, continue on in Literature Circles and book clubs. Small-group discussions expose students to differing points of view, and critical thinking is increased. Students who are less skilled in independent reading are better able to participate in group work and to approach dramatic, artistic, or written tasks with greater confidence.

As students benefit from the shared reading experience, their understanding of who they are, and what they like, and why, increases. And this is why our book collections should be large enough and broad enough to allow students to see themselves reflected as they browse the classroom and library shelves. When a book chooses a student, it is easy for her to step right in. From between the covers, the student's voice can be heard, confident and enthusiastic: "This is a really great book!"

This Books Is Mine

This book is mine.
I checked it out.
I read it
and found all about
another me
who lived before,
who opened up a magic door,
who sailed an ocean,
Flew a plane,
a me
I never could explain
until I found myself
within
a story
where
I've always
been.
— Myra Cohn Livingston, from *I Never Told: And Other Poems*

In the Beginning

"Brian Robeson stared out the window of the small plane
at the endless green northern wilderness below."
From *Hatchet* by Gary Paulsen

After reading this opening sentence from the novel, *Hatchet*, you know three things: (1) a boy is travelling on a small plane, (2) the setting is in the north, and (3) the story is told in the third person. From this lead sentence you know the character's name, a hint of the setting, and the voice that the novel is being told from. Other first sentences might introduce you to the conflict of the story or the relationships between the central characters.

Select a novel to read. Write the first sentence (or up to three introductory sentences) of your novel. Then meet with a partner who has chosen a different novel. The following questions will guide a discussion about the lead sentence of the novel.

Part A: (Paired discussion)

1. What information do you learn from the lead sentence?

2. What question do you have about the novel?

3. What do you predict might happen as the chapter continues?

4. Which novel do you most want to read? Why?

Part B: (Working on your own)

Use the opening sentence of the novel to complete the following items.

1. The lead sentence contains _____ words.

2. The author introduces one or more characters. ___ Yes ___ No

3. The author describes the setting. ___ Yes ___ No

4. The author gives a hint about the conflict in the novel. ___ Yes ___ No

5. The story will be told in the first person, that is,
   from the point of view of "I." ___ Yes ___ No

List three questions you have about the novel after reading the opening.

1. _____

2. _____

3. _____

Are you looking forward to reading this novel? Why or why not?

_____

Pembroke Publishers © 2015 *This Is a Great Book!* by Larry Swartz and Shelley Stagg Peterson ISBN 978-1-55138-308-8

Thinking about Your Novel Program

Considering the following questions will help you to confirm and challenge your assumptions about teaching novels. Check any item that is pertinent to you to help you plan your novel program and then reflect on and revise it for the next year.

☐ How are novels balanced with other parts of your literacy program?

☐ When choosing novels, do you consider students' interests, gender appeal, varied reading developments, and needs?

☐ Are the novels you introduce organized around a theme? an author study? a genre approach?

☐ How are novels part of your reading aloud program?

☐ How much choice do students have in the novels they will be reading?

☐ How much choice do students have in the response activities?

☐ Are response modes (e.g., written, digital, visual arts, drama) varied?

☐ How are media and technology integrated into your novel program? (Consider blogs, wikis, and podcasts of students' critiques, for example.)

☐ How frequently are Literature Circles used to talk about novels?

☐ Throughout the year, do you balance whole-class community reads, small-group, and independent reading of novels?

☐ Do you consider ways of connecting students' outside reading to school activities?

☐ Is there a structured time for daily silent reading in your program? What follow-up strategies, if any, are implemented to have students respond to their reading?

☐ Are reading response journals used as a medium for response? How are students' responses shared?

☐ What methods of assessment do you have in place to track students reading? to assess reading behaviors? to assess response?

☐ How are novels used for mini-lessons and demonstration of comprehension strategies?

☐ Do you share an enthusiasm for reading with your students?

☐ How do you keep up-to-date with newly published novels? (For example, do you look at book reviews or websites, talk with librarians, consult book clubs, or seek student recommendations?)

☐ What is something you would like to change or improve about your novel program?

☐ How would you describe your novel program to others?

☐ What questions do you have about building a better novel program?

Pembroke Publishers © 2015 "This Is a Great Book!" by Larry Swartz and Shelley Stagg Peterson ISBN 978-1-55138-308-8

2

Which Novels for Which Reader

"There is no such thing as too many books."
— Strand Bookstore, New York

Students' interests and tastes, book format, author popularity, the appeal of reading what friends are reading, and the gender of protagonists are all factors in helping to determine what novels readers in elementary school and beyond might enjoy. Before looking at novel options, however, let us consider the kinds of readers that teachers encounter in the classroom.

Who Are the Readers?

Children ages 8 to 15 years old reveal the individualization of both interests and abilities. Their range of reading levels is varied, and their tastes may shift from day to day. Because their lives are busy both inside and outside the classroom, both with print and technology, they may overlook novels unless they have the support of interested adults who are passionate about reading. Although many readers in this age group come to reach a level of independence, media and technological awareness and involvement tend to overshadow independent leisure reading.

Below are profiled various kinds of readers by developmental phase, such as novice, and by challenge, such as being an English Language Learner (ELL).

Transitional, or Novice, Readers: Students who are moving into independent reading but who may not have security with print need high motivation accompanied by accessible material. Students from Grades 3 to 5, who are approaching and developing an engagement with novels, need books that meet their interests and match their ability: books that have the power to immerse them in their stories so that they will complete the books and feel the satisfaction that doing so entails.

Books divided into chapters, with illustrations and much dialogue, are often accessible to those embarking on novel reading, but word count and controlled vocabulary do not ensure success — the search for meaning is what drives young readers to finish a book. It is important that these students not be pushed into reading novels that fail to interest them or that they would find too difficult. It is particularly at this phase of reading growth that successful reading experiences determine their future as readers.

Reluctant Readers: Like novice readers, these readers may need, for a variety of reasons, assistance and encouragement with the novels they are beginning to read. To support their reading and nourish their motivation, teachers may provide opportunities for students to listen to a book, or part of a book, being read on tape, or by an adult, or with a buddy. These students can also benefit from participating in book talks in large-group discussions and Literature Circles. Reluctant readers should be encouraged to work with other students to complete response activities that involve them in revisiting and reflecting on novels.

ELL Readers: These readers face special challenges in the language arts program. Although they may be highly motivated to read, their love of English may not be sufficient to allow them to read the novels they would like — novels with sophisticated plots, character development, and vocabulary — at their emotional and chronological levels of development.

In the past, high-interest, low-vocabulary books tried to address this need; however, their plot lines often failed to satisfy many readers' desire for a "good" book. These students, then, were left with a choice of reading novels below their level, struggling to read novels that demanded a higher level of language capability than they possessed, or reading novels published in their first language that, while fulfilling, did little to promote language growth in English.

Strategies for Reading Development: ELL Readers

Here are some strategies that we can borrow from our practice with reluctant readers as well as specific practices to encourage ELL students in their reading:

- Assign the class paired readers, where an ELL student is paired with another student to read a novel.
- Offer daily read-aloud sessions where reading practices are modeled.
- Have on hand audiobooks that students can listen to as they follow along with a print copy of the book.
- Arrange for a buddy system, where an older student or a proficient reader reads with an ELL student in the class on a regular basis.
- Offer a range of response activities, including art and drama that may not rely on language proficiency.
- Encourage students to work with a partner or in a small group to complete written or verbal response activities.

Good Choice: Supporting Independent Reading and Response, K–6 by Tony Stead (2009) is an excellent resource for helping teachers establish independent reading and borrowing routines.

Developing Readers: Students ages 9 through 12 gain reading power through in-depth experiences with books. Readers who are developing their experience reading novels usually enjoy books by a favorite author or a series about a set of characters. Common themes link the most widely read books: humor, school, friends, mystery, and fantasy. Boys and girls may prefer different types of books; all students may be influenced by the reading choices of their peers. Grades 4 to 6 can be considered to be the "quantity" years where, as novel readers, students strengthen their tastes and interests.

Independent Readers: For students who develop into independent readers, a banquet of novels is available for them to enjoy. These students can find books at an appropriate print and emotional level that will challenge their knowledge, ideas, and concepts. They may prefer to read in depth within a certain genre or to choose novels from a broad spectrum of themes, genres, and formats. Independent readers may be fluent readers who are not ready to move into adult fiction; they can, however, deepen their literary experiences by reading texts of a more challenging nature.

Boys, Novels, and Literacy

"A good book for a boy is the one he wants to read."
— James Moloney, *Boys and Books: Building a Culture of Reading around Our Boys*, page 12

Recommended Resources
- *Even Hockey Players Read: Boys, Literacy, and Reading* by David Booth
- *Reading Don't Fix No Chevys: Literacy in the Lives of Young Men* by Michael W. Smith and Jeffrey D. Wilhelm

The Ontario Ministry of Education addresses the issue of boys and literacy development in these two documents:
- *Me Read? No Way! A Practical Guide to Improving Boys' Literacy Skills* (2004)
- *Me Read and How! Ontario Teachers Report on How to Improve Boys' Literacy Skills* (2009)

Educators such as David Booth and Jeffrey Wilhelm challenge us to conquer the myth that "boys do not like to read." Boys like to read. We need to recognize that many boys in the Junior and Intermediate years immerse themselves in novels that are part of a series. We also need to recognize that boys are immersed in all kinds of reading with all kinds of texts outside school. We can neither ignore the pleasure that many boys gain from information texts nor disregard the world of technology, a significant part of boys' reading lives. In many cases, however, boys do not like to read what they are presented with in our classrooms.

Novels that young male readers are required to read as they mature should connect to their world, in addition to possessing new language, styles, narratives, and themes that contribute to their quality. Booth (2002), author of *Even Hockey Players Read*, advises that when teachers offer a rich and varied mix of books (including fiction) and are mindful of boys' reading preferences, they go a long way towards building engaging and inviting reading environments for boys.

Every reader takes something different from a novel. When boys and girls read the same adventure novels, their attitudes, anticipations, and reactions will be different. Girls, for the most part, respond to the feelings of the characters and how their personalities are shaped by life events and relationships; boys enjoy the action and find that sections that offer description and reflection detract from the story. Girls may read books with boy protagonists, but boys may be reluctant to read books about girls, often based on anxiety about gender images.

Are we perpetuating a stereotype by suggesting that some books are for single sex audiences? It may be so. When it comes to judging a book by its cover, boys are no different from girls: would boys choose to read The Baby-Sitters Club or Princess Academy series? Some would. Today's publishing industry produces a vast range of fiction that could be considered "boy books," books that appeal to what has traditionally been viewed as boys' particular tastes and interests. What is a good book for a boy? What kind of book? What kind of boy?

Is There Reading Life for Boys after Captain Underpants?
Author Reflection

What is the life for boy readers after Captain Underpants? I wonder if my nephew, Matthew, who devoured Dav Pilkey books, the Animorphs series, and the Percy Jackson & the Olympians saga, will move on as a teenager and an adult to get pleasure from books with both female and male protagonists. Will Matthew, despite what statistics inform us about men's tastes, choose to read fiction? What changes will happen in his reading life inside and outside school that will deepen or detour his interest with fiction?

Authors of Special Appeal to Boys

For Transitional and Developing Readers
Max Anderson
K. A. Applegate
Andrew Clements
Jeff Kinney
Gordon Korman
Paul Kropp
Dav Pilkey
Rick Riordan
J. K. Rowling
Louis Sachar
Jeff Smith
Jerry Spinelli
Geronimo Stilton
R. L. Stine
Eric Walters

A Teacher-Librarian's Picks by Genre

"Teachers can recommend novels within the genres of fiction that students already prefer. Here are just a few examples. Humor readers may read *The Brilliant World of Tom Gates* (Roald Dahl Funny Prize) by Liz Pichon and then read *Milo: Sticky Notes* and *Brain Freeze* (New York Public Library 100 Books for Reading and Sharing, 2010) by Alan Silberberg, or *Flora & Ulysses: The Illuminated Adventures* (Newbery Medal) by Kate DiCamillo. Historical fiction readers may read the series I Survived by Lauren Tarshis and then read *September 17* (Silver Birch nominee) by Amanda West Lewis. Fans of horror may read Goosebumps by R. L. Stine and then *Coraline* or *The Graveyard Book* (Newbery Medal) by Neil Gaiman, or *The Night Gardener* (Silver Birch winner) by Jonathan Auxier."
— Mary Catherine Doyle

As teachers, we have sincere interests in laying the yellow-brick reading-roads of our students, step by step, book by book, page by page. If we discover the real reading interests of boys, our classroom programs will then need to accommodate their preferences and needs. Like the girls they sit alongside in our classrooms, boys need to make choices in their literacy lives and develop a sense of ownership of their reading selves. When we understand and accept the differences of boy and girl readers, we can review our reading environments and consider whether we discourage boys from being engaged as readers, or whether we guide students into the reading paths where they can meet books they might or might not meet on their own and which might or might not happen to be novels. *L.S.*

Credit: A version of this article titled "Is There Life after Captain Underpants? Fiction for Transitional Boy Readers" by Larry Swartz first appeared in *Beyond Leveled Books: Supporting Early and Transitional Readers in Grades, K–5*, second edition, by Karen Szymusiak, Franki Sibberson, and Lisa Koch (2008).

The Kinds of Books That Many Boys Like to Read

- Books that are funny
- Books that appeal to a sense of mischief
- Books that focus more on plot and action than description
- Books that invite them to solve problems along with the characters
- Sequels that sustain engagement and invite them to discover what's up with characters they have come to care about
- Books that are visual
- Books that describe other worlds, other times
- Books that reflect an image of themselves
- Books that their friends like to read

Many boys aren't the only ones who enjoy books like these — many girls do, too!

Classifying Novels by Genres and Themes

Any lack of books in the classroom should not prevent readers from embarking on a wide reading program. Everyone can have at least one school or public library book. Many young people also make purchases from local bookstores or from book club offerings, and begin personal collections. They could draw on these titles for their independent reading. Students need to be given as many opportunities as possible to choose novels for their reading. They need, according to Tony Stead (2009, 4), "to discover the many purposes of reading and to become active participants in the selection process."

Regardless of the developmental phase, gender, or context of the reader, students will make their novel choices from among the genres and themes described in the chart that follows on pages 30 and 31. Key aspects of various kinds of novels, along with a number of model novels, are identified.

An Overview of Novel Genres and Themes

ADVENTURE NOVELS

- Exciting, fast-paced plot more important than characters or theme
- Swiftly moving action with characters pursuing clearly stated goal
- Often take the form of a journey

The Terrible Thing That Happened to Barnaby Brocket by John Boyne
The Phantom Tollbooth by Norton Juster
The Mysterious Benedict Society (series) by Trenton Lee Stewart

ANIMAL STORIES

- A mix of animals and humans
- Naturalistic wild animals
- Anthropomorphic creatures

The Underneath by Kathi Appelt
Julie of the Wolves by Jean Craighead George
Silverwing (trilogy) by Kenneth Oppel

BIOGRAPHICAL NOVELS

- Written as if it is about a person's life
- Can be written by someone else or by protagonist
- Despite fictitious characters, form shares similarities with biographies, autobiographies

Our Canadian Girl (series)
White Lily by Ting-Xing Ye
Run by Eric Walters

DIARY NOVELS

- Written as private account of protagonist
- Story told as though novelist (protagonist) is unaware that anyone will read the diary

The Dork Diaries (series) by Rachel Renée Russell
Mabel Riley: A Reliable Record of Humdrum Peril and Romance by Marthe Jocelyn
The Amazing Days of Abby Hayes (series) by Anne Mazer

FANTASY NOVELS

- Imaginative, alternative world ruled by created laws and values
- Though set in the realm of magic, laws are consistent, credible
- Often inhabited by supernatural or mythical creatures

The Glass Sentence by S. E. Grove
His Dark Materials (trilogy) by Philip Pullman
The Thief Lord by Cornelia Funke (Also: *Dragon Rider, Inkheart, Inkspell*)

GRAPHIC NOVELS

- Format easily recognizable by storyboard or comic-book presentation
- Story told through illustrations and dialogue balloons, with some narration
- Multi-genre approaches, including adventure, fantasy, and humor

El Deafo by Cece Bell
Bone (series) by Jeff Smith
Smile by Raina Telgemeier (Also: *Drama, Sisters*)

HISTORICAL NOVELS

- Teach history by telling story of people who lived in a past time
- Incorporate historical facts, although characters and events may be imaginary
- Provide authentic picture of another time

The Underground Railroad by Barbara Smucker
Stones for My Father by Trilby Kent
Tales from Big Spirit (series) by David Alexander Robertson

HORROR NOVELS

- Supernatural/unnatural events, creatures
- Possess brooding atmosphere of terror
- Combine an eerie setting, violent acts, and display of powerful forces

The Night Gardener by Jonathan Auxier
Coraline by Neil Gaiman (Also: *The Graveyard Book*)
Cirque du Freak (series) by Darren Shan

HUMOROUS NOVELS

- Are both funny and fun to read — intent is to make reader laugh
- Enable readers to live out fantasies by reading about adventures they wish they could have
- Appreciation dependent on personal taste

A Barrel of Laughs, a Vale of Tears by Jules Feiffer
Flora & Ulysses by Kate DiCamillo
The Day My Butt Went Psycho (trilogy) by Andy Griffiths

ISSUES/PROBLEM NOVELS

- Deal with topic issue/problem in a serious or candid manner
- Provide insights into the way people think and act

Speak by Laurie Halse Anderson
All the Bright Places by Jennifer Niven
Chandra's Secrets by Allan Stratton

MYSTERY NOVELS

- Create suspense, with atmosphere as an important element
- Usually involve a protagonist and an antagonist
- Are plot oriented with a problem to be solved

Chasing Vermeer by Blue Balliet
The Eye of the Crow: The Boy Sherlock Holmes (series) by Shane Peacock
The Tom and Liz Austen Mysteries (series) by Eric Wilson

REALISTIC FICTION

- Deals with the "here and now"
- Allows readers to identify with issues of behaviors and experiences
- Relationships, friendships, and social attitudes and values predominate

Out of My Mind by Sharon Draper
The Fault in Our Stars by John Green
The Crazy Man by Pamela Porter

SCIENCE FICTION

- Features scientific facts, hypotheses, and technology to present other worlds, times
- Speculates about possibilities of real and future worlds
- Shows similarities between fictional and real worlds deliberately in order to lead reader to consider the world from a new point of view

The Keeper of the Isis Light (trilogy) by Monica Hughes
The Girl Who Owned a City by O. T. Nelson
The Eye of Minds by James Dashner

SPORTS NOVELS

- Appeal to readers interested in sports and sports heroes
- Usually examine the effect of competition on an athlete
- May appear as part of a series by one author

The Crossover by Kwame Alexander
Comeback Kid (series) by Mike Lupica
Lorimer Sports Stories (series)

VERSE NOVELS

- Written in free-verse poetry
- Usually written in first-person voice
- Narrative built through a series of poems, each not more than two pages

Home of the Brave by K. A. Applegate
Love That Dog by Sharon Creech
Out of the Dust by Karen Hesse

WAR NOVELS

- Rely on setting as an important part of the story
- Teach historical facts about countries at war
- Gain readers' sympathies for a protagonist trapped by an enemy

Private Peaceful by Michael Morpurgo
Sunrise over Fallujah by Walter Dean Myers
Code Name Verity by Elizabeth Wein

A Continuum of Novels: From Chapter Books to YA Fiction

In this section, we discuss specific titles within the various kinds of novels that students encounter at different times during their evolution as readers. We look at chapter books and at fiction for transitional readers, developing readers, and young adult readers. Therefore, our continuum recommendations are organized according to these four sections:

1. Chapter Books (ages 7 to 9)
2. Fiction for Transitional Readers (ages 8 to 11)
3. Fiction for Developing Readers (ages 9 to 12)
4. Fiction for Young Adults (ages 12 to 15)

In addition to the discussion of titles within this chapter, there are clear, organized lists of the titles on pages 121 to 123 for ease of reference.

How We Made Our Choices

"A Constellation of Authors" (see page 33) is a graphic that highlights more than 100 Canadian, American, and international authors for both students in Grades 3 to 6 and Grades 7 to 9. The center of the Venn diagram identifies authors who are popular with both younger and older readers.

As authors, we have both been responsible for providing book lists for courses that we have taught, workshops we have given, and articles and publications highlighting the world of children's literature. For this professional resource, we have taken a fresh opportunity to revisit titles from our bookshelves and to think about the hundreds of books we have read as both classroom teachers and university instructors. In recommending titles and providing lists, we have endeavoured to be as expansive as possible in order to include as many favorites as possible.

Nonetheless, in choosing the titles you see below in this chapter, we are aware that some students, teachers, librarians, and parents will think: "How could they not include . . .?" Any librarian, bookstore owner, reviewer, professor of children's literature, and interested parent will have book choices of their own to recommend. And, of course, the students of any generation expect to see their own must-have titles on any recommended lists.

So, we had several questions to consider, these among them:

- Do we choose favorites from decades ago or recent titles?
- How do we best represent different genres and themes?
- How do we represent Canadian as well as international authors?
- How do we represent the popular choices, the award winners, and the well-reviewed titles?
- How do we best classify titles for readers of different age groups and different developmental stages?

What's *Your* Idea of a Great Book?

We respect anyone's choices that differ from ours and welcome the recommendations of any reader who has the joy of saying "This is a great book!" In Activity 2-6 (on page 60), students have a chance to devise lists of their own.

In the end, the titles featured in this section, and this resource as a whole, are *our* choices, and the choices are authentic. Between the two of us, we have read all of the books noted (although maybe not all titles in a series). Choosing from the thousands of novel titles that have appeared since we began teaching, we appreciate that we are considered to be experts in the field. Sorting out and recommending great books has been challenging, but rewarding.

First, though, we acknowledge that some books are deemed to be classics, or books that consistently appeal to readers for generations.

A Constellation of Authors

Grades 3 to 6

Lloyd Alexander	Kathy Kacer
Katherine Applegate	E. L. Konigsburg
Natalie Babbitt	Madeline L'Engle
Betsy Byars	Gail Carson Levine
Matt Christopher	C. S. Lewis
Beverly Cleary	Jean Little
Andrew Clements	Anne M. Martin
Eoin Colfer	L. M. Montgomery
Karen Cushman	Phyllis Reynolds Naylor
Roald Dahl	Barbara Park
Kate DiCamillo	Shane Peacock
Deborah Ellis	Daniel Manus Pinkwater
Louise Fitzhugh	Pamela Porter
Paul Fleischman	Cynthia Rylant
Jean Fritz	Louis Sachar
Patricia Reilly Giff	Jon Scieszka
Morris Gleitzman	Richard Scrimger
Lisa Graff	William Steig
Andy Griffiths	Mildred Taylor
Kevin Henkes	Cynthia Voight
Polly Horvath	David Walliams
James Howe	Laura Ingalls Wilder
Dick King-Smith	Eric Wilson
Brian Jaques	

Grades 4 to 9

Avi
Judy Blume
John Boyne
Sharon Creech
Christopher Paul Curtis
Paula Danziger
Jack Gantos
Gordon Korman
Lois Lowry
Katherine Paterson
Gary Paulsen
Richard Peck
J. K. Rowling
Pam Muñoz Ryan
Marsha Skrypuch
Jerry Spinelli
Eric Walters
Jacqueline Wilson

Grades 7 to 9

David Almond	Anne McCaffrey
Ann Brashares	Farley Mowat
Susan Cooper	Walter Dean Myers
Robert Cormier	Donna Jo Napoli
Brian Doyle	Kenneth Oppel
Lois Duncan	Francine Pascal
Marian Engel	Shane Peacock
Anne Fine	Kit Pearson
Paula Fox	Rodman Philbrick
John Green	Tamora Pierce
Karen Hesse	Philip Pullman
S. E. Hinton	Arthur Slade
Monica Hughes	Mildred Taylor
Ursula LeGuin	J. R. R. Tolkien
David Levithan	Tim Wynne-Jones
Robert Lipsyte	Jane Yolen
Kevin Major	Paul Zindel

Classics: Books That Hold Their Own

A comprehensive list of recommended Canadian book titles appears in the magazine *Best Books for Kids & Teens*, published by the Canadian Children's Book Centre.

Some novels can be considered classics because their characters, storylines, and themes are timeless. Regardless of the era in which they were written, these books say something about the enduring essence of growing up that young people recognize and so the books still become part of young people's experiences, and are treasured and found on many bookshelves today. E. B. White's *Charlotte's Web*, Frances Hodgson Burnett's *The Secret Garden*, L. M. Montgomery's *Anne of Green Gables*, C. S. Lewis's *The Lion, the Witch, and the Wardrobe*, and Philippa Pearce's *Tom's Midnight Garden* are among such titles. To some degree, too, classics enjoy renewed life through the generations by being recast as movies or plays. Consider, for example, Tolkien's *The Hobbit* and *The Lord of the Rings* — the special effects of today's multimedia world can give characters a contemporary sheen.

Every classic was once a new book, and it is likely that classic titles are those that parents are most familiar with. Students' parents may be nostalgic about titles read during their childhoods, remembering both the pleasure of the text and the context of the reading. Were they read to while sitting alongside a parent? Was a book a gift? Was it an independent choice from the library? Was it a title enthusiastically shared by a teacher? Adults may be eager to share books that are personal favorites, but many young people may get caught up in the current tastes and trends of their peers. It is possible that classics will not speak to members of a generation with modern sensibilities. Still, opportunities for reading aloud a classic (or part of a classic) may ignite an interest and, therefore, build a connection between an adult, a book, and a reader. Often, classics hold their own as they sit side by side with the best of contemporary literature. And some contemporary novels will likely become tomorrow's classics!

Consistent Choices

Each year for our children's literature courses, we invite beginning teachers to list novels that they fondly remember from their own years sitting in classrooms from Grades 4 to 8. No matter the group, several titles are sure to appear on the list, thus representing "classic" choices.

Tuck Everlasting by Natalie Babbitt	*Hatchet* by Gary Paulsen
James and the Giant Peach by Roald Dahl (and other titles)	*Holes* by Louis Sachar
	Maniac Magee by Jerry Spinelli
The Outsiders by S. E. Hinton	*The Hobbit* by J. R. R. Tolkien
The Giver by Lois Lowry	*Charlotte's Web* by E. B. White
Bridge to Terabithia by Katherine Paterson	

Stepping Stones — Chapter Books (Ages 7 to 9)

Chapter books are the stepping stones for young readers into the world of novels. The distinguishing features of chapter books are the short chapter format (often with a title for each chapter), the inclusion of a number of illustrations, and somewhat larger print than the books these readers will meet later.

As children learn to read sequential chapters that create a complete story, they are given a chance to anticipate and predict — the major thinking operations in reading. When seven- to nine-year-olds choose chapter books, it indicates that these readers are now able to sustain their interest over several chapters, making sense of plot and characters as the information builds up. As the incidents and images in the books grow one upon the other, the children build a larger framework for understanding. They may come to realize the pleasure and satisfaction that come from "a longer read."

What is most significant is that the chapter books that young readers encounter usually belong to a series by one author. Many children at this young age like to collect things, and series books are another way for children to build collections. Because they take the guesswork out of choosing something to read, books in a series are easily accessible. The familiarity of the characters, the comfort of a recognizable author's style, and the enjoyment of a theme, such as mystery or humor, combine to form a strong appeal for these young readers.

Many characters in chapter books experience school lives similar to those of the children who read the books. Readers can connect to these characters at the same time as they are amused by their cartoon-like fictional behaviors. Young girls, in particular, are enraptured reading about Barbara Park's feisty Junie B. Jones and her adventures in Kindergarten and Grade 1. Similarly, many young girls come to consider their own world of friendships, adventures, and misadventures with such girl heroes as appear in *Clementine* by Sara Pennypacker, *Ivy & Bean* by Annie Barrows, *Judy Moody* by Megan McDonald, and *Nancy Clancy* by Jane O'Connor. Boys, more than girls, seem to enjoy reading the witty tales of *Marvin Redpost* by Louis Sachar or *Jake Drake: Bully Buster* by Andrew Clements. The popular aardvark characters in the Arthur picture book series by Marc Brown have moved on to appear in Arthur chapter books, enjoyed equally by boys and girls. Similarly, The Kids of the Polk Street School and New Kids at the Polk Street School by Patricia Reilly Giff, The Pee Wee Scouts by Judy Delton, and The Adventures of the Bailey School Kids by Debbie Dadey and Marcia Thornton Jones allow readers to enter the neighborhoods and join the clubs of these popular story characters.

Just as many adults enjoy getting wrapped up in a good mystery that challenges them to follow the clues and diversions laid out by the author, children enjoy mystery stories. This genre provides an authentic context for them to look for meaning and synthesize information. Children who enjoy reading Nate the Great stories by Marjorie Weinman Sharmat might move on to meet the girl with a photographic memory in the Cam Jansen series by David Adler and then read about Donald Sobol's mastermind Encyclopedia Brown in stories that challenge them to get involved in solving cases along with a police chief's son. Like the popular adult series by Sue Grafton, Ron Roy's A–Z Mysteries is a collection of mystery stories each with an alphabetically sequential alliterative title (e.g., *The Absent Author*, *The Bald Bandit*); his books, however, are for young readers.

Adventure stories have a strong appeal to transitional readers of novels. The series My Big Fat Zombie Goldfish by Mo O'Hara, Beast Quest by Adam Blade, and Screech Owls by Roy MacGregor satisfy a taste for exploration and discovery and imagined experiences that the fictional world can provide. In Flat Stanley's Worldwide Adventures, created by Jeff Brown, students can travel far and wide through such titles as *The Mountain Rushmore Calamity*, *The African Safari Discovery*, and *The Japanese Ninja Surprise*. Frieda Wishinsky's Canadian Flyer Adventures describe the time-travel trips of characters Emily and Matt: *Crazy for Gold*, *Danger, Dinosaurs!* and *Yikes, Vikings!* are three titles in this series.

Both the Magic Tree House series by Mary Pope Osborne and the Time Warp Trio series by Jon Scieszka invite children to hop aboard the pages of a book and travel to another time, another place. The dozens of titles in these two adventure series have helped children activate their prior knowledge of the world and learn about history and geography. At the same time, young readers come to learn how the world of fiction relies on the suspension of disbelief as the imagination is ignited. Children can choose to read these books sequentially in the order they were written or select particular topics and settings that appeal to them. Both these adventure series are episodic and usually involve the protagonists in working to solve problems in the world in which they are trapped. For example, in *Mummies in the Morning* (Magic Tree House #3), Jack and his sister are whisked off to ancient Egypt, where they encounter a long-dead queen who needs their help. In *Tut Tut*, the Time Warp Trio travel back in time and find themselves in a weird predicament involving a young pharaoh named Thutmose and his evil minister, Hatsnat.

Another fictional trip to Egypt occurs in the book *The Mummy with No Name*, a title in the best-selling Geronimo Stilton series of more than 40 titles. Geronimo is an Italian-speaking mouse who works for a fictional newspaper and goes around the world getting into trouble and solving problems. The books, authored by Geronimo Stilton (a pseudonym for Elisabetti Dami), are written as though they are autobiographical adventure stories by Geronimo Stilton. Some titles include *The Phantom of the Subway*, *The Mona Mousa Code*, and *Field Trip to Niagara Falls*.

The Draw of Series — Fiction for Transitional Readers (Ages 8 to 11)

Children in Grades 3 to 6 represent a great range of reading abilities. Yet their common need is to read widely and often. A large selection of books is necessary for children who are novice novel readers moving on from chapter books. These children are beginning to read books independently but may lack some comfort with print; they need a combination of high motivation and accessible material. Transitional readers require interesting books written at a level they can handle. Children at this age often want books that are short or episodic so that they can read them over a short time, yet enjoy the status of reading "thicker" books. These students, in particular, need books with stories in which they will want to be immersed, so that they feel the satisfaction and pleasure of reading. Books written with a controlled vocabulary but little art will seldom impel a child to continue reading.

During the transitional years, boys and girls gain reading power through their experiences with books. Learning to read a series of sequential chapters that create a complete story gives these readers a chance to anticipate and predict: the major operations in reading. Novels for these students mark a reading plateau because young readers can sustain their interest over several chapters, making sense of plot and characters as information builds up. As the incidents and images in the books, particularly series books, grow one upon the other, novice readers build a large framework for understanding that may be carried into future novel reading.

Reading a series of books continues to be a draw for many readers who are eager to discover more about familiar characters. The transition from chapter books to easy-to-read novels can be identified by these features:

- a decrease in the print size
- fewer illustrations
- increased book length

Students beginning a journey with novels enjoy the familiar plot structures of series and take comfort in their key characters such as Ramona, Aldo Applesauce, Amber Brown, Abby Hayes, and the Baby-Sitters Club. Popular authors at this stage include Judy Blume, Beverly Cleary, Andrew Clements, Roald Dahl, Shannon Hale, Gordon Korman, Dav Pilkey, and Lemony Snicket. Once students have read and enjoyed one or two books by a popular author, they tend to want to read other books by that author. Young readers will likely continue this pattern until they are tired of the formula or experience a change in reading tastes.

Although not technically creating a series, many authors will write one or more sequels to engage young readers. Gordon Korman, for example, has authored a number of survival trilogies that are episodic and filled with suspense: Dive, Everest, Island, and Kidnapped. Many books feature animals with anthropomorphic characteristics — children who enjoyed reading *The Mouse and the Motorcycle* by Beverly Cleary usually go on to read *Runaway Ralph* and *Ralph S. Mouse*. Avon, a snail, and Edward, an ant, become friends who go on an adventure (on a tree branch) to find out about the excitement and meaning of life in Avi's *The End of the Beginning* and its sequel, *A Beginning, a Muddle, and an End.* The animal characters in *The Cricket in Times Square* by George Selden reappear in *Tucker's Countryside* and *Harry Kitten and Tucker Mouse*; and the same vampire rabbit and his friends have nocturnal adventures in *Bunnicula, The Celery Stalks at Midnight, Howliday Inn,* and *Nighty Nightmare* by James Howe. Other collections feature characters that are the same age, in similar family situations as the children who read the books, but with humorous out-of-the-ordinary adventures that are the stuff of fiction. Mordecai Richler's fictional hero Jacob Two Two appears in *Jacob Two Two Meets the Hooded Fang* and *Jacob Two Two and the Dinosaur.* For more than 30 years, children have fallen in love with Judy Blume's Peter and his bothersome brother in *Tales of a Fourth Grade Nothing, Superfudge, Fudge-a-Mania,* and *Double Fudge.*

Many novels continue to tickle the funny bones of young readers because of the extraordinary events depicted in them. The adventures of the wacky characters we meet in each chapter of *Sideways Stories from Wayside School* by Louis Sachar are a perfect example of exaggerated humor: the rather bizarre characters include Mrs. Gorf, with her long tongue and pointed ears, and John, who can read words when standing upside-down. Most young people at this age would likely howl at the hilarious episodic events presented in *The Giggler Treatment* by Roddy Doyle. In this wacky story we meet the baby-size Gigglers whose fur changes color as they move and whose mission in life is to "poo on the shoe" of any adult who is mean to children. Other examples of laugh-out-loud, out-of-the-ordinary adventures include *Lulu and the Brontosaurus* by Judith Viorst, which presents the rascally Lulu in the first of her escapades with animal companions; *Chocolate Fever* by Robert Kimmel Smith, about a boy breaking out in brown bumps with the world's first case of chocolate fever; *How to Eat Fried Worms* by Thomas Rockwell, in which a young boy makes a bet with friends to eat 15 worms in 15 days; and *The Nose from Jupiter*, the first book in a series of four by Richard Scrimger, about a young boy discovering that an alien is living inside his nose.

Other books for this age group have a strong appeal because the humor becomes a bit darker or ruder. Leading the parade are the books by Roald Dahl. Most children (and adults) can recall a favorite Dahl book they have enjoyed, perhaps *James and the Giant Peach, Charlie and the Chocolate Factory,* or *The*

Twits, because of the sinister characters, fantastic settings, and remarkable adventure described within.

A Series of Unfortunate Events by Lemony Snicket (aka Daniel Handler) and the heroic adventures of Dav Pilkey's Captain Underpants (with bizarre titles such as *Captain Underpants and the Attack of the Talking Toilets*) have helped the children's book industry explode. These are books that children devour and often want to own for themselves.

Many novels for this age group begin to engage children with real-life problems and may describe strong relationships with pets or animals in the community. Jean Little addresses the concerns of young children by writing about problems with peers, making friends, and overcoming fears. In *Different Dragons*, a Labrador retriever named Gully helps a young boy overcome his fears of dogs and of sleeping alone in the dark; in *Lost and Found*, a young girl nervous about making friends in her new neighborhood becomes enamored with a stray Maltese terrier. *Stone Fox* by John Reynolds Gardiner describes a race between a boy and his sled dog, and an Aboriginal man named Stone Fox. A flock of wild geese help a young boy deal with his problems in *Jacob's Little Giant* by Barbara Smucker; similarly, swans help a young boy with mental challenges learn to cope in *Summer of the Swans*, and a fox helps a lonely boy grow stronger in *The Midnight Fox*. These last two titles are both by Betsy Byars.

At this age, realistic fiction begins to represent the world the children live in at home and at school, and authors begin to help readers contemplate the complexities of building friendships and finding their place in the family. Many readers can identify with Kevin Henkes' Billy Miller (*The Year of Billy Miller*) who starts school with a bump on his head and worries about best friends, his sister, bats, and rainy days. Set in the past, Newbery Award–winning *Sarah, Plain and Tall* and its sequels, *Skylark*, *Caleb's Story*, and *More Perfect Than the Moon*, invite young readers to cheer for children their age who have experienced loss and learn to adjust to having a new parent. In *Edward's Eyes*, Patricia MacLachlan creates a stirring portrait of a boy who loves music, books, and baseball. When Edward unexpectedly dies, his parents donate his eyes so they can give sight to another boy. *The Jacket* by Andrew Clements depicts a school incident involving a hand-me-down jacket that forces a white boy to become aware of racial discrimination and prejudice when he looks to his father for advice. Coping with death is a central theme in *A Taste of Blackberries* by Doris Buchanan Smith, *Mick Harte Was Here* by Barbara Park, *Sun & Spoon* by Kevin Henkes, and *Missing May* by Cynthia Rylant.

From Quantity to Quality — Fiction for Developing Readers (Ages 9 to 12)

Grades 4 to 6 are the quantity years, when children broaden their reading interests and tastes and may begin to build their own book collections. Many fine books have been written with this audience in mind. Children enjoy reading several books by a favorite author or in a popular genre. Giving them as many opportunities as possible to choose the books to read on their own is important. Boys and girls may prefer different types of books.

For children who are developing into mature, independent readers, many novels available at an appropriate print and emotional level will also challenge their concepts and ideas. Rather than moving to more difficult or adult fiction, these children need to deepen their reading experiences by beginning to choose

Although much of what we teach in school is based on learning facts and acquiring information, incorporating literature helps to inform students' feelings and connect their feelings to intellect, thus creating a strong impact.

quality alongside quantity. Novels from other countries, other cultures, or other contexts can present these young readers with problems and situations of greater complexity, subtle characterization, and multifaceted plot structures. These children can read the novels that represent the best of fiction for children.

Fiction for readers in this age group continues to revolve around these themes: friends, family, fantasy, humor, sports, mystery, adventure, nature, and contemporary issues. These universal themes represent the interests and concerns of pre-adolescents: peer groups, their place in the social system, and the complexity of growing up. Even the most fantastical of novels reveals an underpinning of real situations and problems.

For many children in Grades 4 to 6, novels provide road maps for the challenges of contemporary life. They can identify with and live through the exploits of the fictional characters and learn about many aspects of life vicariously, all while having enriching literary experiences. Since good books are forms of art, the perceptions and views built up through novels can give children a strong affective and cognitive basis for life, as well as a secure grounding in literacy. *Bridge to Terabithia* by Katherine Paterson broke ground in highlighting a special friendship between a boy and a girl, and many novels have since featured strong male and female protagonists who grow and learn from each other. A troubled boy and his mother, and a man and his lonely daughter, come together in a run-down motel in *Greetings from Nowhere* by Barbara O'Connor. As the characters try to help the widow who must sell her home, they hope to create a brand-new life for themselves. In Jerry Spinelli's *Eggs*, nine-year-old David forms a friendship with a quirky, independent 13-year-old girl named Primrose. Despite their differences, David and Primrose form a tight friendship as they help each other deal with coming from broken homes. *If a Tree Falls at Lunch Period* by Gennifer Choldenko alternates between the viewpoints of Kirsten and Walk, seventh-graders at an elite private school. These two friends help readers to consider how race, wealth, weight, and other issues have an impact on friendships when they are faced with a mean but influential classmate.

At this age, boys and girls can make strong emotional connections to the books they read, particularly with characters who feel like outsiders or who have special needs to deal with. Lisa Graff delves into the world of the child who feels like an outsider whether it's Albie, a boy with learning disabilities (*Absolutely Almost*), the orphaned Cady (*A Tangle of Knots*), or Trent, living with the guilt of accidentally killing a boy after shooting a hockey puck (*Lost in the Sun*). In *The Thing about Georgie*, Georgie is small — a dwarf, in fact — and in this novel by Graff, the hero needs to overcome his small stature and his fears of becoming a not-so-big older brother. Although she wants a "normal" life, in the novel *Rules* by Cynthia Lord, 12-year-old Catherine learns to cope with a brother with autism and a family that revolves around his disability. The "rules" that introduce each chapter give Catherine strength as she comes to understand the answer to the question "What is normal?" A funny and heartwarming character named Joey Pigza gives readers a compassionate understanding of what it's like to be a learner with special needs in *Joey Pigza Swallowed the Key*, the first book in the series by Jack Gantos. Sequels include *Joey Pigza Loses Control*, *What Would Joey Do?* and *I Am Not Joey Pigza*.

Many students become more sophisticated and emotionally connected to stories about boys and girls who come up against tough circumstances and seek a place to belong both in their family and school circles. *Mockingbird* is a strong, sensitive story by Kathryn Erskine where we meet Caitlin, a young girl with

Asperger's syndrome who is struggling to deal with the loss and tragedy of her brother being killed in a school shooting. Dealing with loss is also part of the world of Willow Chance, a gifted adolescent who is obsessed with diagnosing medical conditions in *Counting by 7's* by Holly Sloan. Two important titles help readers get into the heads of those who are differently abled. Readers of this age can come to admire Melody, a gutsy girl with cerebral palsy (*Out of My Mind* by Sharon Draper), for her strength and fortitude as she strives daily to overcome her disabilities and the misconceptions that go with them. In the must-read book *Wonder* by R. J. Palacio, readers accompany August Pullman, a boy born with extreme facial abnormalities, into his first year in school and come to understand the challenges of building friendships, wanting to fit in, and being just "ordinary."

Just as students of this age group reflect on their relationships in school and community, they also give careful thought to their own families and their places in them. A wide range of family situations are portrayed in novels for independent readers in Grades 4 to 6. Deirdre Baker's *Becca at Sea* describes the adventures of a young girl who visits her grandmother's cottage while her parents prepare for the arrival of a new baby. Georgina, the heroine in *How to Steal a Dog* by Barbara O'Connor, lives with her overworked mother and younger brother in the family car in a small town in North Carolina. Desperate to help her mother improve the family situation, she solicits the help of her brother to get money by stealing a dog and then claiming the reward that she thinks the owners are bound to offer. In *Jakeman* by Deborah Ellis, the bus to Wikham Prison carries Jake and his older sister Shoshona, along with a group of other unhappy kids, all anxious to see their mothers. Tired of being bossed around and following orders, Jake hatches a plan to find the Governor and plead with him to pardon their moms. In Susan Patron's *Higher Power of Lucky*, 10-year-old Lucky Trimble is determined to run away when she finds out that her legal guardian might abandon her. In *Mother Number Zero*, Marjolijn Hof sensitively describes the issues that surround adoption. In the verse novel, *42 Miles* by Tracie Vaughn Zimmer, JoEllen needs to decide where her loyalties lie as she tries to bring together her two separate lives — one as Joey, who enjoys weekends with her father, and another as Ellen, who lives with her mother in an apartment near her school and friends. *A Monster Calls* is a powerful, haunting read about a 13-year-old boy who dreams about monsters — and confronts a monster who helps him to understand and cope with the truth of his mother's dying of cancer. This novel, written by British author Patrick Ness, was inspired by an idea from Siobhan Dowd and is accompanied by stark black-and-white illustrations created by Jim Kay.

Developing readers also tend to seek out books that are funny, and humor becomes more sophisticated and wry in the novels for this age group. Any visit to a bookstore will reveal large displays of graphic-format readers such as the series *Diary of a Wimpy Kid* by Jeff Kinney, *Dork Diaries* by Rachel Renée Russell, and *Nate the Great* by Marjorie Weinman Sharmat. In the companion novels *Everything on a Waffle* and *One Year in Coal Harbour*, Primrose Squarp sharply observes family, friends, and strangers in the West Coast community in which she lives. *Flora & Ulysses* brought Kate DiCamillo another Newbery Award for the hysterical adventures of a girl, a squirrel, and a vacuum cleaner. *Flora & Ulysses* is humorous not just because of the story and the way that DiCamillo tells it but also because of the illustrations and comic-strip format that appear throughout the novel. *Audrey (Cow)* is a funny book told by a funny cow and her funny animal friends in a not so funny adventure about a cow that tries to escape the fate of being slaughtered. Readers who enjoy a good laugh are easily lured by such titles as *The Day My Butt Went Psycho, Zombie Butts from Uranus*, and *Butt Wars! The Final Conflict*, epic tales of a boy and his crazy runaway butt. (Really!) Beyond that, David Walliams has caught the baton from Roald Dahl to write books that are so funny, somewhat twisted, and often just a bit gross. Even the titles of Walliams's books inspire a smile and invite delight: *Mr. Stink, The Boy in the Dress, Gangsta Granny, Demon Dentist, Billionaire Boy*, and *Ratburger*.

Although not intentionally funny books, humor filters through many stories with characters that the students might easily identify with. Readers may recognize themselves in these books or believe that the author has taken a camera into their classrooms. Andrew Clements is the ideal author of mishaps, often amusing, that take place in classrooms: series include The School Stories and Keepers of the School; among his engaging novels are *Frindle, The Landry News, The Janitor's Boy*, and *No Talking. Because of Mr. Terupt* by Rob Buyea presents a year in the life of a fifth-grade classroom. The book is framed around 10 months of the school year, and in each month the viewpoints of seven students are featured as they carefully reflect on the day-to-day happenings in school as well as the engaging lessons learned from their teacher, Mr. Terupt, whom each fondly admires. The laughter and learning with teacher and students continues in two sequels: *Mr. Terupt Falls Again* and *Saving Mr. Terupt*. Jennifer Holm celebrates the wonder of science and questions the aging process and the possibility of immortality in *The Fourteenth Goldfish*, the story of a girl, a scientist, and a departed goldfish.

Many developing readers are still interested in books with animal characters. Many of the stories they read are told in the first person, thereby endowing the animal with human-like characteristics and emotions whether it's a mouse (*Abel's Island* by William Steig), a horse (*War Horse* by Michael Morpurgo), a gorilla (*The One and Only Ivan* by K. A. Applegate), or a dog (*Ellie's Story* and *A Dog's Purpose* by W. Bruce Cameron). In fact, books about dogs, such as the Shiloh trilogy by Phyllis Reynolds Naylor and recent releases such as *Rain Reign* by Ann M. Martin, have huge appeal to readers of this age. Gordon Korman pokes fun at the predominance of dogs in his novel *No More Dead Dogs*, knowing that books such as *Sounder* by William H. Armstrong, *Where the Red Fern Grows* by Wilson Rawls, and *Stone Fox* by John Reynolds Gardiner may bring tears to the eyes of readers young and old, and will be read over and over again throughout the decades.

Adventure stories set in different time periods — such as *The Castle Corona* by Sharon Creech, *Crispin* by Avi, *Alex and the Ironic Gentleman* by Adrienne Kress, and *Escape from Mr. Lemoncello's Library* by Chris Grabenstein — engage readers with their plot twists and exotic settings. Bob Barton takes readers on a fantastic Arctic journey on a Northwest Passage expedition, based on true events. *Trouble on the Voyage* is both the title of his novel and the central conflict in this survival story told through the eyes of 11-year-old Jeremy, a ship's boy trapped along with the ship's crew in Hudson Strait. In *The Mysterious Benedict Society* by Trenton Lee Stewart, an 11-year-old boy reads an advertisement for "gifted children looking for special opportunities" and sets out on a series of challenging and creative tasks as part of a group of four. Author Rick Riordan has taken hundreds of thousands of young readers on fictional adventures with the commercially successful Percy Jackson & the Olympians and Heroes of Olympus series, presenting the world of Roman and Greek mythology to young readers, as well as The Kane Chronicles, centered on Egyptian mythology. Riordan also helped to launch The 39 Clues mystery adventure series, where each title is written by a different author. Fantasy worlds à la Harry Potter and fantasy characters continue to be enormously popular with boys (and girls) in the middle years, particularly as series books: Artemis Fowl by Eoin Colfer, Animorphs by K. A. Applegate, Warriors by Erin Hunter, and *Charlie Bone: Children of the Red King* by Jenny Nimmo.

See the discussion on multicultural books on pages 48 to 51.

A wide range of cultures and religions are portrayed for developing readers, often providing a mirror to their own lives and a window into identities that may be different from their own. In order to help students of this age become respectful citizens, it is important to provide them with books that will allow them to understand the backgrounds, customs, and identities found in multicultural books. It is as they become young adolescents that students are ready to be empathetic to the plights of others. For example, *Esperanza Rising* by Pam Muñoz Ryan introduces readers to a young girl who is forced to leave her family ranch in Mexico when tragedy hits. When Esperanza and her mama flee to a California camp for Mexican farm workers, the girl is not prepared for the hard labor and lack of acceptance she faces. In *Iqbal* by Francesco D'Adamo, readers learn about a life of poverty in Pakistan, where Iqbal is sold into slavery in a carpet factory. In *The Breadwinner* by Deborah Ellis, students learn about a life of poverty in Afghanistan where Parvana, who is forbidden to earn money as a girl, transforms herself into a boy to become the breadwinner for her family. Cynthia Kadohata won the Newbery Medal for *Kira-Kira*, which chronicles the move that Katie and her family took from a Japanese community in Iowa to the deep south of Georgia. Katie and her sister Lynn are struck by the stares of the people who pass them on the street, but it is Lynn's illness that forces the family to come together. The Newbery Medal also went to Linda Sue Park for her novel *A Single Shard*, set in 12th-century Korea. In this book we meet an orphaned boy named Tree-ear who, through an accident, becomes mentored in the art of making pottery. Park's *A Long Walk to Water*, based on a true story, tells about the lives of two 11-year-olds in Sudan, each searching for their families and a safe place to stay.

Themes That Resonate — Fiction for Young Adults (Ages 12 to 15)

Novels for readers ages 12 to 15 years old allow young people to engage in a dialogue with the author on a wide range of topics at a deep emotional level. The personal and private reading of a novel gives young people the security to delve into situations that may reflect their lives, giving them opportunities to identify and reflect upon human traits and behavior. The themes of these novels reflect the development of young adolescents, their concern about their place in the adult world, social justice, peace, ecology, the future, and the past. Young adolescent readers, striving to understand life's problems, come to accept the portrayal and examination of these issues, carefully and artfully developed in the novel, in order to strengthen their understanding and beliefs of their own world and of society. Because of their well-developed reading abilities and mature interests, some adolescents may want to move into adult novels at this stage.

"We aren't what we read; we read what we are, and what we can become."
— David Booth, *Caught in the Middle*, page 31

Peer acceptance is at the center of adolescence, and many authors for this age group help students reflect on the complexities of coming of age. It could be argued that more girls than boys are drawn to the realistic fiction written for this age group. The popularity of series books such as The Sisterhood of the Traveling Pants by Ann Brashares and The Clique collection by Lisa Harrison represent the tastes of many girls. An interesting approach to the rollercoaster ride of high school is taken in Lauren Myracle's The Internet Girls Collection, told entirely in instant messages: titles in this series include *ttyl, ttfn,* and *l8r, gr8r.*

Beyond these popular books, many authors of the past four decades show that they are in tune with the young adolescent spirit. Several authors have carried the torch of Judy Blume (*Are You There, God? It's Me. Margaret?* and *Forever*), who needs to be recognized for providing a significant turning point in the novel industry by writing about young people with real problems who face the complexities of growing up. Some authors who have maintained popularity over the past 30 years include Paula Danziger (*The Cat Ate My Gymsuit*), Cynthia Voight (*Homecoming*), Frances Lia Block (*Weetzie Bat*), and Paul Zindel (*The Pigman*).

Recent winners of the Newbery Medal draw on the lives of young adolescents who question their identities and examine their place in the world. Titles include *Moon over Manifest* by Clare Vanderpool, *When You Reach Me* by Rebecca Stead, *Criss Cross* by Lynne Rae Perkins, and *Dead End in Norvelt* by Jack Gantos. There are also recommended Canadian authors of novels for students 12 years and up who deal with family and peer relationships: these include Martha Brooks (*Queen of Hearts*), Julie Johnston (*Adam and Eve and Pinch-Me*), and Marthe Jocelyn (*Would You*).

See "Celebrating an Author through Close Study and Response" and the feature, "Passing On a Love of Stories" by Eric Walters, in Chapter 1, pages 15 to 19.

Although many of the protagonists in this genre happen to be girls, we can learn much about the behaviors, attitudes, and relationships of 12- to 15-year-old boys by reading works by some of Canada's leading male authors, including Eric Walters. Walters is one of the most prolific of these authors, and *Stars, Shattered*, and *Say You Will* exemplify contemporary realistic fiction for males. Walters, in partnership with Deborah Ellis, wrote a novel told from two points of view. In *Bifocal*, Haroon (whose parents emigrated from Afghanistan) is a serious student, devoted to his family. Jay, a white boy, is the school's football star. Readers are taken inside a high school torn apart by racism when the police arrest a Muslim student on suspicion of terrorism.

Christopher Paul Curtis, the author of *The Watsons Go to Birmingham — 1963* and *Bud, Not Buddy*, is another leading Canadian author. Curtis has written *Bucking the Sarge*, about a 14-year-old youth who keeps his sense of humor while running the Happy Neighbor Home Group for Men and dreaming of going to college and becoming a philosopher. A fine example of historical fiction is *Elijah of Buxton*, also by Curtis, which introduces readers to a first-generation freedom child from the Black community of Buxton, Ontario. When the town's corrupt preacher steals money intended to buy the freedom of slaves still trapped in the United States, the hero of Curtis's novel sets off in pursuit of the thief. In a companion novel, *The Madman of Piney Woods*, Curtis further explores the dreams and adventurous nature of adolescent boys.

Tim Wynne-Jones addresses such themes as metamorphosis into manhood as teenage boys deal with survival, terror, grief, and mystery. His titles include *The Maestro*, about a teenage boy who takes refuge with a famous musician in the wilderness of Northern Ontario, *Stephen Fair*, *The Boy in the Burning House*, and *A Thief in the House of Memory*.

A particular strength of several of the novels by male authors is a strong sense of place and culture. Brian Doyle paints a picture of living in Ottawa in the late 1940s in *Up to Low, Angel Square, Easy Avenue*, and *Mary Ann Alice*. Kevin Major sets his books in Newfoundland, offering forthright language and strong characterization in such books as *Hold Fast* and *Far from Shore*.

Any discussion of novels for 12- to 15-year-olds needs to consider the topic of love and sexuality. Leading the parade, as well as many bestseller lists, is author John Green. *Paper Towns* and *Looking for Alaska* portray the trials of falling in and out of love. Green's *The Fault in Our Stars* explores the world of 16-year-old Hazel, who faces new realities and relationships, when she discovers she has cancer. Romance between teenagers who may or may not have things in common can be explored by reading about Stewart and Ashley in *We Are Made of Molecules* by Susin Nilson and *Eleanor and Park* by Rainbow Rowell. Profoundly moving is the story of Finch and Violet who rely on each other to get them through each day — and through life — in *All the Bright Places* by Jennifer Niven. David Levithan's book, *Every Day*, asks whether we can really love someone regardless of their outside appearance in the unique story about a teenager who wakes up every morning in a different body. Levithan also offers important and sensitive insights into homosexual love in his novels *Boy Meets Boy, Two Boys Kiss*, and *Will Grayson, Will Grayson*, which he co-authored with John Green. A special kind of boy relationship is celebrated in two novels: *The Art of Being Normal* by Lisa Williamson, the story of David Piper who hides a truth that he wants to live his life as a girl, and *I Am J* by Cris Beam, on a similar theme. In 2004, *Luna* by Julie Anne Peters was the first young adult novel with a transgender character to be released by a mainstream publisher. In fact, more writers and publishers have begun tackling the transgender subject for middle and young adult readers with voices of transgender youth, such as Alex Gino in *George* and Ami Polonsky in *Gracefully Grayson*, arguing that many young people question their gender identity and that teachers and families should discuss the subject.

Novels about teenagers in trouble, or with rebellious attitudes, are a strong lure for young adolescent readers. Written in 1967, S. E. Hinton's *The Outsiders* is about two brothers who live on the wrong side of the tracks and must come face to face with the privileged "socs." This novel, which the author wrote while she was still in high school, is just as popular today as it was more than 40 years ago. After enjoying S. E. Hinton's first book, many readers (boys, in particular) go on to read other books by the author, including *Rumble Fish, Tex*, and *That Was Then, This Is Now*. In *Slake's Limbo*, Felice Holman tells the story of a troubled teenager who chooses to live on his own in the tunnels of the subway system. Walter Dean Myers brings a contemporary approach to troubled teenagers, specifically Black American boys: in the award-winning *Monster*, 16-year-old Steve Harmon is on trial as an accomplice to a murder; in *Shooter*, three troubled teenagers are involved in a high-school shooting; and in *Autobiography of My Dead Brother*, written by Myers and his son Christopher, the focus is on teen gang violence, and sketches and comic strips are used to help the character make sense of the loss of a close friendship.

The rebel appears in many forms. Jerry, the hero in Robert Cormier's novel *The Chocolate War*, becomes one of the first antiheroes in young adult literature when he finds himself caught between a tyrannical priest and a secret gang leader. Phillip, a ninth-grader in *Nothing but the Truth* by Avi, challenges teacher authority and gets suspended from school because his humming of "The Star Spangled Banner" is seen as disrespectful. Cole Matthews, in *Touching Spirit Bear* by Ben Mikaelsen, must choose between prison and the Native American Justice Circle as his punishment for smashing the skull of another boy. In *Trouble*, Gary D. Schmidt tells the story of 14-year-old Henry, who runs away from home to hike Maine's Mount Katahdin with his best friend and dog. Along the way he meets up with Cambodian refugee Chay Chouan, who had been accused of fatally injuring Henry's brother, and who reveals the trouble that predates the accident. Holling Hoodhood, from *The Wednesday Wars*, is another one of Schmidt's antiheroes. During the 1967 school year, this seventh-grader stays behind in his teacher's classroom while all his classmates go either to Catechism or Hebrew School.

Reading the plays of William Shakespeare, Holling learns valuable lessons about the world he lives in.

J. K. Rowling, with her world-creating imagination and wonderful concrete images, revolutionized the reading world of children's literature with the wizardly Harry Potter. Many adolescents are consolidating their tastes and enjoy reading novels that take them into fantastical worlds, and there is still a strong need at this age for readers to read more than one book in a series. Sitting alongside Harry Potter titles, books by J. R. R. Tolkien, Terry Brooks, Anne McCaffrey, and V. C. Andrews can be found on thousands of teenagers' bookshelves. The Inheritance Trilogy by Christopher Paolini describes the world of a 15-year-old dragon rider whose quests are guided by an ancient storyteller. The His Dark Materials trilogy by Philip Pullman and the Bartimaeus Sequence by Jonathan Stroud take the reader into parallel worlds where demons and mythical creatures live alongside humans. Garth Nix's fantasy trilogy includes modern and medieval worlds in *Sabriel* and its sequels, *Liarel* and *Abhorsen*. Nix's talents as a fantasy writer can also be found in the spirit world of The Seventh Tower series and The Keys to the Kingdom collection, in which a young boy discovers a strange key that is central to saving the world from horrible plagues and sinister characters.

Always ready to be entertained and shocked, many young adults favor books of the supernatural and horror and magic: Septimus Heap by Angie Sage, The Edge Chronicles by Paul Stewart and Chris Riddell, *Cirque du Freak* by Darren Shan, and Protector of the Small quartet by Tamora Pierce. *The Flowers in the Attic* by V. C. Andrews is the first of a series of books that frighten and delight. In this vein, *Miss Peregrine's Home for Peculiar Children* and its sequel, *Hollow Café*, grab the attention of readers with an abandoned orphanage, a collection of old photographs, and the appearance of some very strange characters. Vampires certainly inhabit young adult reading time, with particular thanks to Stephanie Meyer (The Twilight Saga) and *Vampire Academy* by Richelle Mead.

Teenagers facing a series of trials appear in a number of books. These include *The Maze Runner* and *The Mortality Doctrine*, both by James Dashner, and *I Am Number Four* by Pittacus Lore. Strong heroines who survive in alternative futuristic societies have helped boost 21st century book sales for young adults: *The Hunger Games* by Suzanne Collins, *Divergent* by Veronica Roth, and *The Selection* by Kiera Cass.

A Theme That Spans the Novel Continuum: Bullying

Great books can entertain. Great books can educate. Great books can also help readers deal with challenging themes by making connections to the circumstances created by an author and by asking questions about a character's behaviors. Whether part of an up-close look, as when explored in the classroom, or read independently, novels can also enable students to discover and uncover caring and uncaring relationships, such as those that characterize bullying.

The statistics are irrefutable. The headlines are frightening. The stories are painful. The issue of bullying plays a strong part in the culture of today's schools as educators struggle to help young people build better relationships. If we want to help young people live with integrity, civility, and compassion, then we need to introduce strategies and resources that help students come to an understanding of the complex issue of bullying. We need to help students understand why a bully behaves the way he or she does, and we need to provide students with strategies so that they will be prepared if caught in the bully web. Reading and discussing literature are powerful tools for such preparation.

For Younger Readers

In chapter books such as *So Long, Stinky Queen* by Frieda Wishinsky, *Jake Drake: Bully Buster* by Andrew Clements, and *Shredderman: Secret Identity* by Wendelin Van Draanen, young readers learn what it is like to survive the mean people who may be in their classrooms.

Three short novels describe the impact of bullying on children. *Scrambled Eggs and Spider Legs* by Gary Hogg explains what happens when a bully is assigned to be a project partner with the boy who is intimidated by him. In the short British novel *The Angel of Nitshill Road* by Anne Fine, a guardian angel helps three terribly unhappy children who are relentlessly bothered by a bully. In Katherine Paterson's *The Field of Dogs*, not only does a child named Josh have to deal with a bully when his family moves to a new neighborhood, but his dog faces a bully of his own.

Being overweight provides the impetus for bullying in a few key books. Judy Blume, the queen of realistic fiction, wrote one of the strongest books on mean relational and verbal bullying with *Blubber*. The story centers on the teasing endured by an overweight girl named Linda and another girl's growth as she learns that this kind of mean behavior is wrong. A comparative situation can be found in *Larger-Than-Life Lara* by Dandi Daley Mackall, who frames the story in a clever format. Using the writing techniques she has learned in school, a fourth-grader relates how an obese girl in class changes the lives of those around her, despite being bullied by her peers. On the somewhat similar theme of sticking out, *Fatty Legs* by Christy Jordan-Fenton and Margaret Pokiak-Fenton tells the true story of a young Inuit girl who becomes the laughingstock of the residential school she attends because of her thick stockings.

Two novels written more than 40 years ago still meaningfully address the bullying issue. With no friends and a family that seems to ignore him, Martin Hasting, the bully in *The Bully of Barkham Street*, realizes that he must do something to improve his reputation. Mary Stolz helps readers get inside a bully's head and see how a sixth-grader's world looks through Martin's eyes. In *Veronica Ganz* by Marilyn Sachs, readers meet a girl bully. Bigger and meaner than everyone else, Veronica meets her match when shrimpy Peter Wedermeyer tries to gain power within the class.

For Developing and Fluent Readers

The titles of several novels for students from Grades 4 to 6 capture the themes of bullying for both developing and fluent readers. *Starting School with an Enemy* by Elise Carbone, *Bystander* by James Preller, and *The Present Takers* by Aidan Chambers each paint a picture of targets who are being tormented by scary kids.

Author Jerry Spinelli knows exactly what it's like to think and feel like a student in the middle-school years, and each of his books conveys the complexities of peer pressure and the challenges of being accepted. In *Wringer*, Palmer, who is coming of age, must accept the violence of being a wringer in his town's annual pageant or find the courage to oppose it. In *Stargirl*, a new girl in the school dares to do things her own way, challenging those around her to consider what is normal. In *Loser*, Donald Zinkoff exemplifies a kid who seems to rise above it all, as his optimism, exuberance, and the support of his loving family prevent him from feeling like the misfit his classmates view him as.

R. J. Palacio's *Wonder* is an important title to recommend for the bullying theme since the heroic August Pullman, born with a facial deformity, needs to confront bullies at his school who have little empathy or compassion for his quest to be "ordinary."

The bully issue is also explored in vivid stories by Canadian authors. Aaron, in *Better Than Weird* by Anna Kerz, Will Reid, in *Egghead* by Caroline Pignat, and Henry K. Larsen, in *The Reluctant Journal of Henry K. Larsen* by Susin Nielsen, are three brave souls who are tormented even though they try to fly under the radar of bullies in their school. Newfoundland author Jill MacLean has written a trilogy: *The Nine Lives of Travis Keating, The Present Tense of Prinny Murphy*, and *The Hidden Agenda of Sigrid Sugden*. Each title can be read separately, but reading all three can help mature readers come to understand the complex relationships between the bully, the bullied, and the bystander, especially those who live in a small community.

For Young Adult Readers

For young adolescents, the issue of the bully, bullied, and bystander triangle helps readers carefully consider the relationships in their own lives. *The Misfits* by James Howe is about a group of four students who do not seem to fit in with their small-town middle school. When it is time for school council elections, the students join together to represent all students who have ever been called names. In Nicky Singer's *Feather Boy*, a strong story about a class target named Robert is told. When a strange senior citizen calls upon Robert to help solve the mystery of a derelict house, Robert learns what courage it takes to find his own voice and never give up. A teacher plays an important part in *The Skin I'm In* by Sharon G. Flake: the new teacher at the school helps Maleeka learn to be comfortable with herself.

The bullying problem, of course, continues in high-school settings, with novels sometimes addressing the consequences. When three popular girls go on trial in government class for their ruthless bullying of a classmate, everyone has to come to terms with the fallout. One book, *Poison Ivy* by Amy Goldman Koss, is presented as eight first-person narrators giving different versions of the same event. Legal proceedings are essential to the tough story *Tease* by Amanda Maciel, where a young teenage girl faces criminal charges for bullying after the suicide of one of her classmates. When the protagonist in *Inventing Elliot* by Graham Gardner becomes a victim of school bullying, he tries to invent a calmer, cooler persona by changing schools in the middle of the year; however, he soon attracts the wrong kind of attention from a group known as the Guardian, determined to maintain order at the school. Moving to a new school and finding a place to fit in also pose problems for other characters: Butterball, in *Playground: The Mostly True Story of a Former Bully* by 50 Cent with Laura Moser; Miracle Boy, in *Bullyville* by Francine Prose; Todd Munn, in *Scrawl*; and Paul Fisher, in *Tangerine* by Edward Bloor. The power of cliques and their manipulation over others are the foundation of two other novels: *Shattering Glass* by Gail Giles and *Speak* by Laurie Halse Anderson. Finally, a horrific picture of the bullying issue is described in Todd Strasser's *Give a Boy a Gun*, in which two boys, who have been mercilessly teased and harassed by the jocks at their high school, set out to get revenge and gather a small arsenal of guns from a neighbor.

War as a Novel Theme for Young Adults

Novels set in the First and Second World Wars provide much more than information about battles, heroes, and political leaders. Through the relationships, experiences, fears, and hopes of fictionalized young people living in wartime, these novels help readers to see the impact of war on individual children and their families, and the resourcefulness and inner strength that individuals needed to survive during wartime.

Michael Morpurgo is a highly recommended author of novels set during the world wars. Tommo's recollections of his life with brother and fellow soldier, Charlie, lead to a surprising and deeply emotional end in *Private Peaceful*, set in the First World War. Morpurgo's *War Horse* is told from the perspective of Joey, a farm horse sold to the army and later captured as a work horse for the German army. It is a story of friendship, courage, and determination. A remarkable theatre production from the National Theatre in London and a movie version by Steven Spielberg have added to the popularity of this book written early in the author's career.

Elizabeth Wein's *Code Name Verity* is a gritty, suspenseful novel set in England and France during the Second World War. The first half of the book is told from the perspective of Verity, a captured British spy who is handing over information to the Gestapo after a prolonged period of torture. Readers hear about Maddie, her friend and the pilot who dropped her into Nazi-occupied France, in Verity's account, but some of the holes are not filled in until the second half, when Maddie tells her story.

The early days of flight are the setting for John Wilson's *Wings of War*. Gaining flying experience in Saskatchewan thanks to his Uncle Horst, Edward achieves his dream of being a pilot when he joins the Royal Flying Corps in England. His story personalizes the statistics of the battles and loss of lives in the trenches and in the skies during the First World War.

Beyond those titles, several authors have series books for young adults set during the Second World War. These include Chris Lynch (*The Right Fight*: Book 1 in the World War II trilogy) and Canadian authors Kit Pearson (The Sky Is Falling trilogy) and Eric Walters (the Camp X series; see also *War of the Eagles*).

Novels with Alternative Perspectives: Multicultural Books

Multicultural books give voice to individuals and groups whose perspectives have not been widely voiced in children's literature and other publications. Beyond addressing issues of race and ethnicity, these novels encompass characters with disabilities and with differences in religion, sexual preference, socioeconomic status, and so on. In some multicultural books, fictional characters from marginalized groups are placed in powerful positions. In other books, the lives of women and men who have made noteworthy contributions are chronicled. Some multicultural books highlight injustices, often through fictional accounts of real events.

Turn to "Novels on Selected Themes," on pages 124 and 125, for a convenient list of titles on bullying, war, and multicultural themes.

Powerful Positioning of Characters

The following recommended books tend to have been published by small presses. They feature characters who are not part of the dominant socio-political society because of their race, ethnicity, abilities, or sexual orientation.

- In Jean Little's *Willow and Twig*, 10-year-old Willow takes on responsibilities and shows wisdom far beyond her years as a child of a young woman who has long suffered from drug addiction. She is the only one who understands her four-year-old brother, Twig, who has attention deficit disorder and impaired hearing.
- Ruby Slipperjack's *Little Voice*, part of the In the Same Boat series, features Ray, a girl of mixed heritage. Ray's father has been killed in a work accident, and Ray lives with her grandmother in Northern Ontario.
- In Jacqueline Guest's *Outcasts of River Falls*, set in 1901 rural Alberta, intelligent and strong-spirited 14-year-old Kathryn Tourond has moved from Toronto to live with her aunt after the death of her father. There, she comes to know more of her Métis cultural heritage and the racist policies that restricted the Métis from owning land and forced them to live on government-owned road allowances. The action-packed story features a Robin Hood–like highwayman who helps the Métis and is accused of murder.
- Sonia Manzano's *The Revolution of Evelyn Serrano* is set in 1969 Spanish Harlem. The novel brings together three generations of strong women of Puerto Rican heritage who take part in civil rights movements, the Puerto Rican Nationalist uprising of 1937, and the actions of the Young Lords in El Barrio, in New York City, in 1969.
- In two other books, young people take part in anti-government action in totalitarian government contexts. Carolyn Marsden's *My Own Revolution* is set in 1960s Czechoslovakia. In a suspense-filled narrative, 13-year-old Patrik and his friends engage in minor acts of resistance against the Soviet-controlled communist government, and his family makes plans to defect through Yugoslavia to Italy. The repressive dictatorship of Augosto Pinochet in Chile is the context for Marjorie Agosín's *I Lived on Butterfly Hill*. An 11-year-old Chilean girl, Celeste Marconi, is exiled to her aunt's home in the United States as her parents go into hiding because of their political leanings and humanitarian actions in Valparaíso.
- In *Aristotle and Dante Discover the Secrets of the Universe*, Benjamin Alire Sáenz creates two strong characters: Dante, who is confident with his identity as a Hispanic gay adolescent, and Ari (short for Aristotle), a Mexican American. Dante develops a close friendship with Ari during a summer when his father works as a visiting professor at an El Paso, Texas, university. A homophobic beating and an accident where Ari saves Dante's life, injuring himself in the process, add to the complexity of this novel of friendship, sexual awakening, and family relationships.
- Like Ari, Reginald McNight, the Jamaican-American protagonist in Olugbemisola Rhuday-Perkovich's *8th Grade Super Zero*, is a memorable underdog character. After a disastrous first day of school, Reggie tries to keep a low profile. Political activist Ruthie convinces him to join her as a volunteer at a homeless shelter with his church's youth group. Readers will be inspired by this humorous story of Reggie's quest for justice for others and discovery of his own strengths and identity.

- Jason Blake, a 12-year-old with autism in Nora Raleigh Baskin's *Anything but Typical*, finds a friend through an online writing site. Writing allows Jason to interact with his friend in ways that he finds difficult in social settings.

Celebrating Less-Known Remarkable People

A number of multicultural books are fictionalized biographies of people who have made important contributions to their local communities and to the larger society through their courage, strength, ingenuity, and compassion. Because of their race or gender, these people may not be well known. The authors of the fictional biographies introduce young readers to these less-known heroes through their graphic novels and novels. In Tales from Big Spirit, a series of graphic historical novels written by David Alexander Robertson and illustrated by Andrew Lodwick and Scott B. Henderson, a contemporary Aboriginal young person meets up with someone from the past who tells the stories of heroic, notable people from Canadian history. Although some of the names of featured Indigenous men and women are widely known, other names deserve to be better known. The graphic novels in this series celebrate the remarkable contributions of these individuals:

- John Ramsay, who helped settlers from Iceland survive through Manitoba winters, hunger, and a smallpox epidemic, despite having had his land expropriated by the Canadian government
- Tommy Prince, who was renowned for his marksmanship and tracking abilities, and greatly admired for his bravery during the Second World War and the Korean War
- Gabriel Dumont, Métis leader of the Northwest Resistance in the late 19th century
- Shawnadithit, last surviving member of the Beothuk Nation of Newfoundland
- Pauline Johnson, a great poet of the Edwardian era
- Thanadelthur, the courageous peacemaker between the Cree and the Dene and translator for the governor of Fort York

The importance to Black Americans of the 1937 victory of Joe Louis over James Braddock to become boxing champion is the undercurrent in a story by Andrea Davis, *Bird in a Box*. The path Louis took to the world heavyweight boxing champion title is chronicled as three Black American children listen to his fights on the radio.

Another hero, this time of 19th-century Japan, Manjiro, is highlighted in *Heart of a Samurai* by Margi Preus. Manjiro's adolescence, spent on an American whaling ship and in the home of the ship's captain in the United States, provided Manjiro with cultural knowledge and a mastery of English unmatched by anyone else in Japan at that time. The Japanese Shogun, or military leader, deciding to end Japan's 250-year isolationist policy with a peace treaty between the United States and Japan, was heavily dependent on Manjiro and awarded him status as a samurai: the first peasant fisher to gain such a title.

The childhood of Beryl Markham, who flew solo across the Atlantic from England to Canada in 1936, is narrated by Michaela Maccoll in *Promise the Night*. Growing up with her father on a ranch in colonial Kenya, Markham is educated by a prominent member of the Nandi tribe and befriends his son before being sent to a residential urban school for white girls. Adventurous and with a fiercely independent spirit, Markham smashes gender stereotypes — for example, going on a lion hunt — but doesn't always recognize her privilege as a white woman. The complexities of her childhood are revealed in chapters alternating between diary entries and newspaper accounts of Markham's cross-Atlantic flight.

Zora and Me, co-written by Zora Neale Hurston aficionados, Victoria Bond and T. R. Simon, is another fictionalized account of a noteworthy woman's childhood. It is loosely based on documented accounts of the master storyteller's life. With a lively imagination and indomitable spirit, the young Zora and her friend track down a murderer in the all-Black community of Eatonville, Florida, in the late 19th century. Racism is an undercurrent in this suspenseful story.

Fictional Narratives and Memoirs of Historical Injustices and Inequities

Novels about historical injustices and inequities provide young readers with suspense-filled, emotionally engaging stories that also share well-researched information about historical times, events, and issues. The depth of information and insight into the issues provides a wealth of topics for later discussion with peers and the teacher.

Elizabeth Stewart's *The Lynching of Louie Sam* draws on known events that took place in the late 19th century: teenagers George Gillies and Pete Harkness secretly followed a lynch mob that travelled to Canada from Washington Territory to capture and hang 14-year-old Louie Sam from the Stó:lō Nation, who had been wrongly accused of the murder of a local man. This well-researched story provides a chilling account of racism and a historical injustice that has been officially acknowledged only recently.

Injustices of the past are further chronicled in Margarita Engle's *Silver People: Voices from the Panama Canal*. Engle brings readers to the early 20th century when the Panama Canal was being built by "silver people" from Caribbean countries. Housed in boxcars, these people worked in dangerous conditions, resulting in many lives being lost, and were paid in silver. Told in verse from many perspectives, including those of white workers who had better working and living conditions and were paid in gold, this story makes real the human and ecological costs of the canal.

The injustices of more recent times in North America are narrated in *My Name Is Not Easy* by Debby Dahl Edwardson and *Fatty Legs* by Christy Jordan-Fenton. In Edwardson's book, Iñupiaq brothers Luke, Bunna, and Isaac are sent to a residential school in the Alaskan interior, far from their Inuit village. Based on the real-life story of the author's husband and his brothers and told from the perspectives of Luke and five classmates, this story sensitively and honestly portrays life in a residential school in the 1960s. Through the first-person accounts of each of the students, readers see how the racial tensions among the European, First Nations, and Inuit students played out and how the Indigenous students struggled to maintain their identities despite not being able to use their language or even their names. Olemaun (Margaret) Pokiak's memoir was recorded by her daughter-in-law, Christy Jordan-Fenton. The book is titled *Fatty Legs* because of the nickname Olemaun was given when a bullying nun forced her to wear thick red stockings while in a residential school in 1944. At the school in Aklavik, Northwest Territories, Olemaun learned to read and won over another nun who became her champion. She showed resilience and intelligence as she thwarted her tormentor and maintained a proud Inuvialuit (Western Inuit) identity despite the school's assimilationist practices.

Young people surviving the atrocities committed by totalitarian governments are the subject of two recommended novels: *Now Is the Time for Running* by Michael Williams, set in Zimbabwe and South Africa; and *Under a Red Sky* by Haya Leah Molnar, set in communist-controlled Romania. *Now Is the Time for Running* is about two brothers, Deo and Innocent, forced to flee their Zimbabwe home when government soldiers massacre everyone else in their village. As they use their wits to reach Johannesburg, Deo and Innocent are victims of xenophobic attacks against refugees. While practicing and playing on the South African team at the Homeless World Cup, Deo is finally provided with the emotional constancy he needs after years of trauma and loss. As for *Under a Red Sky*, author Haya Leah Molnar relates how it was dangerous to be Jewish in communist-controlled Romania after the Second World War. She was not told by her parents that she was Jewish until she was eight years old. In her memoir, readers learn of the deprivations that she and her family experienced and of their great fears of the secret police; they also learn how family members stayed strong and supported one another, maintaining their Jewish identity.

Hardship and Survival during International and Civil Wars

See the Chapter 4 feature titled "'What Is the Holocaust?' A Literature Circles Approach" by Rachael Stein.

It is as adolescents that readers can begin to grasp the complexities of events that unfolded during the Second World War and in other historical events that have had a critical impact on the modern world. For the historical fiction described in this section, the common purpose of the authors is to expose a part of history by examining the hardships of those greatly affected by international and civil wars, including an effort to help young people understand the horrors of the Holocaust. Such books recognize that many people who read about the past do so to better understand the present and consider the future. Through novels, students can become aware of and understand more deeply the social and political relationships that, across cultures and international borders, have shaped today's world.

- Kathy Kacer's *Hiding Edith* tells the true story of a young Jewish girl, Edith Schwalb, who escapes to Belgium with her family when the Nazis invade Vienna, Austria, in 1938. Photographs taken by one of the orphans, who later became a member of the French Resistance, together with Kacer's sensitive writing, make the horrors of Edith's childhood real to readers.
- In *The Book Thief* by Markus Zusak, Death relates the story of Liesel, a young German girl living in Nazi Germany. The girl's book-stealing and storytelling abilities help sustain her family and the Jewish man they are hiding, as well as their neighbors.
- Jerry Spinelli's *Milkweed* introduces readers to an orphan who lives on the streets of Warsaw and wants to be a Nazi one day. The boy changes his mind when he witnesses the emptying of Jews from the ghettos.
- In *The Boy in the Striped Pajamas* by John Boyne, the horror of the Holocaust is seen through the naïve eyes of Bruno, the son of a Nazi officer who lives with his family in a place he calls "Out-With." Bruno is unaware that the boy he befriends is one of his father's enemies who lives behind a wire fence. A film version of this novel strongly complements the narrative and characterization of Boyne's text.

- At the adolescent stage many students first find that the satiric, autobiographical graphic novels *Maus* and *Maus II* by Art Spiegelman help them understand the impact of surviving the atrocities of war.
- Two novels by Marsha Forchuk Skrypuch chronicle the lives of adolescents separated from their families in the world wars. Skrypuch's *Daughter of War* is about Marta and Kevork, separated by the Turks' deportations of ethnic Armenians during the First World War. Through alternating third-person narratives, readers follow the two as they try to find each other during a time when millions of Armenians were brutally killed. In *Underground Soldier*, 13-year-old Luka escapes from a Nazi work camp and heads to the Carpathian Mountains; there, he becomes a member of the Ukrainian Insurgent Army fighting against the Soviets and Nazis.
- A third novel about atrocities committed against targeted ethnic groups during the Second World War is the acclaimed *Between Shades of Gray* by Ruta E. Sepetys. Fifteen-year-old Lina, her mother, and her younger brother struggle for survival when deported to northern Siberia, where many victims of Stalin's brutal campaign against the Baltic peoples died of starvation, cold, and disease.

Two novels tell the stories of young people whose lives are disrupted in horrific ways because of civil wars in their countries.

- *Bamboo People* by Mitali Perkins tells the story of 15-year-old Chiko, who is tricked and forced into becoming a member of the government army in the Burmese civil war against the Karenni people. Chiko narrates the first half of the book, talking about army life up to the point where he meets with a Karenni boy, Tu Reh; in the second half of the book, Tu Reh is the narrator, presenting another perspective on the civil war.
- Zeina Abirached's graphic novel, *A Game for Swallows: To Die, to Leave, to Return*, takes a very different approach to illustrating a child's life during a civil war. This story takes place on one night in the author's childhood in Beirut, Lebanon, during the civil war of the 1980s. Zeina and her brother fear for their parents, who are returning from a visit with Zeina's grandmother on the other side of the demarcation line between East and West Beirut, and are in danger from the shelling that starts up after they leave. Their fears are eased by neighbors who come to visit and tell stories.

Innovative Novel Forms

See "Novels with Innovative Genre Approaches," on pages 126 and 127, for a convenient summary of titles.

Traditionally, we would consider novels to be arranged in different chapters. Some books have titled chapters; some are structured into different parts. In recent years, many authors have expanded the novel form by presenting the story in different formats. These include verse novels, where the text is written as poems; graphic novels with comic-like formats, where the illustrations and verbal text work together to tell a story; and multi-genre books, which often present more than one writing form, such as list, diary, interview, letter, e-mail, or drawing.

Verse Novels

Many award-winning authors have explored the verse form. Sharon Creech's gem, *Love That Dog*, describes how one young student comes to love poetry by gaining a personal understanding of what different poems mean to him. In the sequel, *Hate That Cat*, we are reintroduced to the characters of Jack and his teacher and the world of poems. In *Heartbeat*, Creech's character contemplates the many rhythms of life the year that her mother becomes pregnant and her best friend becomes distant. Cynthia Rylant's *Ludie's Life* is a collection of poems about the character from childhood, through marriage, motherhood, and old age. Rylant's *Boris* is a tribute to companionship and compassion as seen through the world of a big grey cat. Kevin Major has written a historical novel, *Ann and Seamus*, in poetic form. Author Pamela Porter, winner of a number of Canadian book awards for *The Crazy Man*, presents a story set on the Prairies about the friendship between a girl with a disability and a man with a mental disorder. Jacqueline Woodson describes her experiences of growing up as a Black American girl in the 1960s and 1970s in both the northern and southern United States. In her autobiographical free-verse novel, *Brown Girl Dreaming*, Woodson shares the joys and struggles of finding her voice though writing. She also writes in free-verse style in *Locomotion*, *Feathers*, and *After Tupac and D Foster*. Black American characters are central to two companion stories, *The Way a Door Closes* and *Keeping the Night Watch* by Hope Anita Smith. Finally, *The Crossover* by Kwame Alexander, the 2015 winner of the Newbery Medal, celebrates both basketball and brotherhood.

Karen Hesse, also an award winner, has written several novels in poetry. Hesse won the 1998 Newbery Award for the novel *Out of the Dust*, a rich description of the harsh farm life during the dust storms of the 1930s. With each meticulously arranged verse entry, she conveys a vivid picture of a young girl's desolation, longing, and hope. She uses the same format for the novels *Witness* and *Aleutian Sparrow*.

Novels in poetry lend themselves to reflection. In both *Keesha's House* and *Spinning through the Universe*, Helen Frost weaves together stories of several characters as they struggle to hold their lives together at home and at school. *Frenchtown Summer* by Robert Cormier consists of a series of vignettes in which the writer reminisces about his life as a 12-year-old living in a small town in 1938. The verse form of *Where the Steps Were* by Andrea Cheng details the last year of five Grade 3 students before their inner-city school is torn down. Other school voices are heard in *Naked Bunyip Dancing* by Australian author Steven Herrick, where members of Class 6C come to find out who they are and what they are good at.

The refugee experience is at the heart of a number of novels told in powerful poetic verse. *Home of the Brave*, by Katherine Applegate, tells the story of Kek, an African refugee who arrives in Minnesota to live with his aunt and cousin. Longing to be reunited with his mother, Kek is comforted by new friendships and finds strength in his memories. He develops a sense of responsibility, taking care of a cow that he names Gol, meaning "family" in his African language. Novel chapters are each no longer than four pages. Two books focus on the Vietnamese refugee experience. *Inside Out & Back Again* by Thanhha Lai relates the story of Ha, who has known only the world of Saigon until she is forced to flee. *All the Broken Pieces* by Ann E. Burg focuses on Matt Pin who, while adjusting to his life in the United States with a caring adoptive family, cannot shake the strong memories and secrets of the war-torn country he left behind. *The Red Pencil* by Andrea Davis Pinkney describes the world of 12-year-old Amira in Darfur. More than anything, Amira longs to read and write, but her world is shattered when the militia storm her village.

Several verse novels have been written for teenage readers. *Jinx* by Margaret Wild is a powerful verse novel about identity, loss, and love. Similarly, in *Tricks*, Ellen Hopkins tells the story of five teenagers, rich and poor, gay and straight, who learn about falling apart over love and growing up. The work of Australian author Steven Herrick can be recognized by the poetry that comprises his novels about troubled adolescents: *The Simple Gift*, *By the River*, and *The Wolf*. *The Brimstone Journals* by Ron Koertge presents a haunting series of poems by fictional high-school students who contemplate the violence present in their lives. Martine Leavitt's *My Book of Life by Angel* is a provocative story about a 16-year-old who works the streets of Vancouver.

Multi-Genre Approaches to Novels

Jennifer Rowsell has written extensively about multimodality. Rowsell describes multimodality as a combination of different kinds of modes, such as visual, written, oral, and spatial, in a text's content and design. Modes, she explains, are comprised of the stuff used to create texts.

In today's world, attention is given to making meaning through multimodal ways of presenting information. For example, we can watch, listen to, and read the news on a television screen. Some contemporary authors have taken the opportunity to tell stories through a variety of genres. Among them are Andy Spearman and Sarah Durkee, with titles in a humorous vein. *Barry Boyhound* by Andy Spearman describes a boy who feels and acts like a canine after a flea bite turns his human brain into that of a dog. Skimming through the book, readers can see Spearman's clever use of maps, lists, photographs, exposition, diagrams, captions, a timeline, and scripts that feature conversations between two fleas. In *The Fruit Bowl Project* by Sarah Durkee, a teacher arranges for a rock superstar to teach her Grade 8 students, who each tell a story about the same topic in the style of a rap, a poem, a monologue, a screenplay, haiku, and more.

Many novels are written as diaries. This format provides the opportunity for a story told in first person and invites the reader to learn about the lives of characters from their first-hand views of the world. In The Amazing Days of Abby Hayes series by Anne Mazer, the main character reflects on everyday events, and these thoughts are presented in a different color to accompany Mazer's narrative. Strong heroines tell their stories of the past in diary form in award-winning *A Gathering of Days* by Joan W. Blos, *Catherine Called Birdy* by Karen Cushman, and *Mable Riley* by Marthe Jocelyn.

And journals are not just for girls. *The Diary of a Wimpy Kid* by Jeff Kinney includes cartoon drawings and student print "written" on the lines of a journal. Adrian Mole confronts puberty in the very funny diary novels by Sue Townsend that begin with *The Secret Diary of Adrian Mole, Aged 13¾*. More serious issues are presented in journal format in *Bully Book* by Eric Khan Gale when the character Eric Haskens uses his journal to help him confront those who taunt him. For mature readers, Sherman Alexie wrote *The Absolutely True Diary of a Part-Time Indian*, the story of a teenager named Arnold who laments his life on a Spokane Indian reservation. When a teacher pleads with Arnold to get a better life, the boy switches to a rich white school and becomes as much of an outcast there as he was in his own community. Finally, John van de Ruit uses the journal format for *Spud*, which invites young adult readers into the mind of John "Spud" Milton as he goes through puberty at a South African private school.

The multi-genre approach makes for an interesting twist in reading a novel. In his award-winning book *Monster*, Walter Dean Myers tells the story of the murder trial of a 16-year-old through diary entries, courtroom transcripts, and the teenager's imagined film script, which helps him come to terms with the course his life has taken. In *Shooter*, Myers uses interviews, reports, and journal entries to tell the story of a tragic shooting at a high school. Avi's *Nothing but the Truth* serves as a model for multimodality in a story told through journals, memos, announcements, dialogues, letters, lists, and more.

Electronic communication is represented in a number of new novels, most notably *ttyl* and its sequels *ttfn* and *l8r, g8r* by Lauren Myracle. These books chronicle in instant messaging format the day-to-day experiences and plans of three tenth-grade friends known as the Internet Girls. Michael J. Rosen has written *Chaser* in e-mails to tell the story of a young man who shares his outlook on life when his parents choose to move to a new home in the country. E-mail messages are also spread throughout the novel *The Gospel According to Larry* by Janet Tashjian. There, a 17-year-old creates a secret identity as the author of a website that receives national attention. Battling cancer, a teenage girl tries to complete her classes online in *Sun Signs* by Shelley Hrdlitschka, a novel told through e-email communications. Another novel about dealing with cancer, *Me and Earl and the Dying Girl* by Jesse Andrews, is told through transcripts, lists, and narrative. In this witty book, high-school senior Greg Gaines is forced by his mom to become friends with a girl with cancer in an effort to learn more of what life is all about.

The world of technology is also an important part of the reading experience for the Skeleton Creek series by Patrick Carman. These novels include journal and e-mail messages, but also include links and passwords to a special website that provides clues to solving the mystery of the strange happenings at Skeleton Creek. Hats off to Eric Walters, who presents the wired generation with the novel *Walking Home*, which promotes a variety of text readings. Orphans Muchoki and his sister walk hundreds of kilometres in Kenya to find their last remaining family members. By following the Walters website, readers can explore an incredible digital companion to the reading experience which brings the journey of the Kenyan orphans to life through pictures, maps, videos, songs, and readings.

Novels in Graphic Format

A graphic novel is a type of comic book, usually with a lengthy and complex storyline. Although the format can encompass short story collections, a graphic novel may be described as a stand-alone and complete narrative presented through visual and textual elements. Like a text-only novel, the graphic novel may deal with a complex plot, varied characters and settings, and various subject matters.

Graphic novels deliver a range of genres, from superhero to romance, historical fiction, fantasy, science fiction, and *manga* (the Japanese word for "comic book"). They are closely related to comics in that stories are told with the fusion of sequential picture-frames and written text, but the two genres are distinct. Graphic novels suggest a story that has a beginning, middle, and end, as opposed to an ongoing series with continuing characters. Although the length of graphic novels varies, they are usually longer than comics.

For young readers moving into novels, the graphic novel has a strong appeal because of the use of pictures and more limited text. The Geronimo Stilton series features a variety of fonts and sizes, illustrations, and comic formats to tell the adventures of the rodent journalist. One reason for the popularity of the Captain Underpants series is the comic-strip format, which appeals to many young readers. Even the popular Time Warp Trio series by Jon Scieszka has been transformed into the comic-strip format as has The Baby-Sitters Club by Ann M. Martin. In *Babymouse: Our Hero* by Jennifer L. Holm and Matthew Holm, black,

"By incorporating the graphic novel into school literacy programs, educators will be recognizing students' reading choices outside school and completing them with the texts mandated inside school."
— David Booth and Kathy Lundy, *In Graphic Detail*, page 38

white, and pink images feature an imaginative young mouse who deals with her fears of facing an enemy in a game of dodgeball.

Family relationships, identity, and social acceptance are highlighted in some graphic novels, but the format is particularly suited to fantasy or adventure stories. Among graphic novels featuring relationships and identity are *Harvey* by Hervé Bouchard and Janice Nadeau, *Smile* by Raina Telgemeier, and *El Deafo* by Cece Bell. Books focused on fantasy or adventure include *City of Light, City of Dark*, written by Avi and illustrated by Brian Floca, and entirely in comic-book format. *Travels of Thelonious* by Susan Schade and Jon Buller is an adventure story told in traditional narrative interwoven with graphic-novel storytelling. The Bone series by Jeff Smith, the Akiko series by Mark Crilley, the Three Thieves series by Scott Chantler, and the Leave It to Chance series by James Robinson are popular with, and suitable for, novel readers of various developmental stages in the middle-school years.

When discussing graphic format, it is important to acknowledge the popularity of Japanese *manga*. *Manga*, usually featuring the adventures of superheroes and villains, has exploded the world of novel reading. Series titles include Hikaru No Go by Yumi Hotta, Knights of the Zodiak by Masami Kurumada, Amulet by Kazu Kibiushi, and Prince of Tennis by Takeshi Konomi.

Beyond that, it is interesting to note that several classic novels have been retold in graphic-novel format. These include Tolkien's *The Hobbit* by Dixon Chick, Shelley's *Frankenstein* by Gary Reed, and L'Engle's *The Wrinkle in Time* by Hope Larson.

Powerful stories based on autobiographical events have also made their way into graphic-novel format. *Maus: A Survivor's Tale: My Father Bleeds History*, by Art Spiegelman, was the first graphic novel to win a Pulitzer Prize. The story of a Jewish survivor of Hitler's Europe and his son, a cartoonist who tries to come to terms with his father's story, *Maus* provides readers with gripping details of the Holocaust. Spiegelman continued the theme in *Maus II: And Here My Troubles Began*. Like its predecessor, it is the story of mice characters (Jewish people) and cats (Germans). *Persepolis*, along with its sequels, offers Marjane Satrapi's poignant story of a young girl growing up in Iran and her family's suffering following the 1979 Islamic revolution. The novel is drawn in small black-and-white panels that evoke Persian miniatures. *American Born Chinese* by Gene Luen Yang was the first graphic novel recognized by the National Book Foundation. It starts out with three seemingly different tales, then merges them to present readers with the legendary folk tale *The Monkey King*, a story of second-generation immigration from China, and a perspective on extreme Chinese stereotypes in terms of accent, appearance, and hobbies. This kind of book is more suited to mature young adult and adult readers.

Novels that are heavily illustrated can also be considered graphic in format. Artist Christopher Myers has supplied black-and-white sketches and comic strips throughout *Autobiography of My Dead Brother*, a book about gang violence written by his father, Walter Dean Myers. With *The Invention of Hugo Cabret*, Brian Selznick expands the novel form to create a new reading experience: the book features 284 pages of original pencil drawings. It combines elements of picture book, graphic novel, and film to tell a story about an orphan, a clock keeper, and a thief in the city of Paris, filled with secrets and mystery. In 2008, this novel earned the Caldecott Medal for best illustrated book.

Professional Resources

For further support with graphic texts, check out these titles:

- *Learning to Read with Graphic Power* by David Booth and Larry Swartz
- *In Graphic Detail* by David Booth and Kathleen Gould Lundy
- *Going Graphic: Using Graphic Novels to Promote Literacy with Preteens and Teens* by Michele Gorman
- *Teaching with Graphic Novels* by Shelley Stagg Peterson
- *Adventures in Graphica: Using Comics and Graphic Novels to Teach Comprehension, 2–6* by Terry Thompson

Ten Activities with Graphic Novels

Response activities for graphic novels can be somewhat different than for other types of novels, since responses should invite students to pay attention to the text features inherent in the graphic format.

1. **Identify text features of a graphic novel.** Graphic novels combine the elements of narrative, speech, illustrations, and images that seem to move on the page into a reading experience that is unique. Students can become familiar with the text features by researching such terms as *panel, gutter, panel border, word balloons, thought bubbles,* and *caption boxes.*

2. **Illustrate panels that might be added into a page of a graphic text.** In this way, the reader is making inferences about what might happen in between scenes. By creating images the reader is also developing the comprehension strategies of sequencing, visualizing, and making predictions.

3. **Dramatize stories.** Graphic stories are ideal for dramatization, since students can become the characters on the page and say the words written in the speech bubbles. Challenge them to represent the different scenes/panels as closely as possible to the words and images featured. Groups can present the story in sequential order, frame by frame.

4. **Present both the narration and dialogue of a story as Readers Theatre.** Since the focus of Readers Theatre is the words, the use of gestures and props is kept to a minimum. Once students have identified their parts (one or more can be assigned to read the narration), they can practice different ways to say the words.

5. **Prepare a script.** Students can transform the dialogue from a scene in a graphic novel into a script for performance. In this way, they can consider different ways that dialogue can be written.

6. **Go on a font hunt.** A change in font, a change in size, or the use of color brings different meaning to the story. Invite students to examine a section of a graphic text and list different ways that verbal text has been featured. Students can discuss why they think the text has been represented in each way.

7. **Explore how balloons are used.** Students can list and sketch different ways that speech balloons are used in a graphic novel. Discussion can focus on these questions: What are some different shapes and sizes of speech balloon used by the author? Why do you think the author made these different choices?

8. **Retell a graphic story in a group.** One person tells the story and the other group members ask questions to clarify the story. The activity can be done in or out of role. Alternatively, students can sit in a circle, with each group member, in turn, contributing to the storytelling. Encourage them to include many details to describe the sights, sounds, conversations, and events from the novel.

9. **Consider points of view shown in illustrations.** Students can examine different ways that scenes have been illustrated to tell a story and establish a mood, and look for close-up, middle-distance, and long-distance scenes. They can then choose one panel and draw it from a different viewpoint than the artist has chosen.

10. **Transform an excerpt from a novel not presented in graphic style into graphic format.** Students will need to make decisions about narrative captions, word balloons, settings, and points of view to tell the story in graphic detail.

Reflecting on Reading Choices: Activities

The following six activities, some of which involve the use of line masters, invite students to think about why they make the reading choices they do. Teachers can choose one or more of the following to help draw students' attention to the key issue of choice and to have students take an inventory of the choices and preferences of their novel reading.

Activity 2-1: Factors in Book Choices

Provide students with a copy of the line master "Factors Influencing Novel Choice" (page 61). Students can place a check mark beside any item that they feel influences their reading choices. To help them prioritize, invite students to put an asterisk (*) beside three choices that are the most influential. Survey the class to find out which factors are the most popular. Students can discuss reasons for their choices.

Activity 2-2: Whose Opinion Matters?

Challenge the students to rank the following six possible influences on how they make choices in reading:

friends, websites, a teacher, a librarian, book reviews, themselves.

Most important is #1; least important is #6. If they wish, they may add items to the list.

Once they have prepared their lists, prompt them to meet with other students to compare their rankings. Students could also take an opportunity to share any book titles that have been recommended to them. You could survey the class to determine which factors most influence students' choices.

Activity 2-3: Would You Rather . . . ?

Students can approach the opinionnaire "Would You Rather . . ." (page 62) in one of two ways. They can complete the form, which is intended to help them consider their preferences for reading, independently, or they can work in pairs, interviewing each other. Students can then work with three or four classmates to compare answers. As teacher, ask students to consider these questions: "Who answered most similarly to you? Was there a perfect match with anyone?" Finally, choose one or more of the items from the "Would You Rather . . .?" line master and survey the class to find out the most popular choices.

Activity 2-4: Read Anything Good Lately?

Direct each student to prepare a list of all the print texts read in the last 48 hours. Lists may include books, magazines, social media connections, and environmental print. Once their lists are completed, have students put a star beside the reading that they spent the most time with; a check mark beside any item that was "assigned"— in other words, not read by choice — and a dot beside their most unusual or special reading experience. In groups of four or five, let students share their lists and discuss. Which items are similar? Which are unique to individual students? Who spent the most time reading?

Activity 2-5: My Great Book Bookshelf

Activity 2-5 is inspired by *My Ideal Bookshelf*, a book in which authors Thessaly La Force and Jane Mount present the thoughts of cultural figures who share the titles of books that have mattered most to them.

The line master "My Great Book Bookshelf," page 63, provides students with an opportunity to consider books that are important to them. Students fill in the spines with different titles of appropriate books — they are not limited to novels. The same line master can be used at different times of the year as a tracking sheet for students to record novels they have completed reading.

Extension: Invite students to choose at least one of the titles and write a description of the book, explaining why it is important to them.

Activity 2-6: Top 10 Lists

Suggest that students put a number of age-appropriate titles from this list on a To Read list.

This activity invites students to study the "Leisure Reading List of Top 10 Titles" (pages 119–120) and consider some of their own choices. In groups of two or three, students review the list and identify the titles they are familiar with.

Tell the students that the list represents titles that its two authors mutually agreed upon after some discussion and negotiation. They worked together to prune their own favorites to the specific lists of just 10 items featured on the line master (they did, however, manage to slip in a few more favorites or sequels in parentheses). What are some titles that students might add to any of these top 10 lists? One criterion for the lists is that the books had to have been published since the year 2000.

There are, however, many great books from the 20th century and earlier, too. Many of these are classics that the students or their parents will have been introduced to. Tell students to work alone or in the same small groups as above to prepare a top 10 list of classic titles from the 20th century (and, if they wish, before) that they would recommend for independent reading.

Factors Influencing Novel Choice

Place a check mark to the left of any item that you feel influences your reading choices. You might also put a little star (*) beside the three factors that influence your choice of novel the most.

- ☐ **Level of Difficulty:** Is the novel too easy? too challenging? just right?

- ☐ **Length:** Is the novel too long? too short? just right?

- ☐ **Format:** How appealing is the shape of the book? the size of the print? the font? the length of chapters?

- ☐ **Author:** Is the author familiar? Is she or he popular?

- ☐ **Series:** Is reading about familiar characters in familiar situations an appealing idea to you?

- ☐ **Interests:** Are the story and setting familiar? What knowledge will you gain by reading this book?

- ☐ **Availability:** Is the book one of yours, or does it belong to the classroom? a library? a friend?

- ☐ **Situation:** Will you read the book independently? as part of a small group? as part of a larger group?

- ☐ **Issues:** What can you learn about personal conflicts? social conflicts? political conflicts?

- ☐ **Cultures:** What can you learn about personal identity? the identity of others?

- ☐ **Setting:** Is the setting modern? historical? in the future? in another country? in a place of interest?

- ☐ **Genre:** Is this genre familiar to you? Would this be a typical choice for you?

- ☐ **Popularity:** Is the book popular with other students?

- ☐ **Gender Appeal:** What gender is the protagonist? Is the book free of stereotypes?

- ☐ **Cover:** How appealing do you find the title? the illustrations? the colors? the blurb? the review comments?

- ☐ **Recommendations:** Has the book been recommended by a teacher? a parent? a friend? a librarian? a bookstore owner? a relative?

Pembroke Publishers © 2015 *"This Is a Great Book!"* by Larry Swartz and Shelley Stagg Peterson ISBN 978-1-55138-308-8

Would You Rather . . . ?

Complete this opinionnaire to consider some of your reading preferences. Aim to make only one choice for each of the 10 items. Another way to approach this is to find a classmate as a partner and take turns interviewing each other. You could mark up a copy of the opinionnaire as your partner offers an answer.

1. Would you rather read . . .
   a) more fiction than non-fiction?
   b) more non-fiction than fiction?
   c) fiction and non-fiction equally?

2. Would you rather . . .
   a) subscribe to a magazine?
   b) buy a novel?
   c) borrow books from the school or community library?

3. Would you rather . . .
   a) read news online?
   b) read a newspaper?
   c) watch the news on television?

4. Would you rather . . .
   a) read a hardcover novel?
   b) read a paperback novel?
   c) read an e-book?

5. Would you rather . . .
   a) read a novel that is 400 pages or more?
   b) read a novel that is between 200 and 400 pages?
   c) read a novel that is less than 200 pages?

6. Would you rather . . .
   a) read a novel that is funny?
   b) read a novel that is historical?
   c) read a novel that is fantastical?

7. Would you rather . . .
   a) read a biography or an autobiography?
   b) read a how-to information text?
   c) read a novel in either traditional or graphic format?

8. Would you rather . . .
   a) read something recommended by a teacher or librarian?
   b) read something recommended by a friend?
   c) read something you chose yourself?

9. Would you rather . . .
   a) read a novel and then see the movie?
   b) see the movie and then read the novel?
   c) just read the book or just see the movie?

10. Would you rather . . .
    a) read novels that are in the same series?
    b) read different novels by the same author (not series)?
    c) read novels by a variety of authors?

Pembroke Publishers © 2015 *"This Is a Great Book!"* by Larry Swartz and Shelley Stagg Peterson ISBN 978-1-55138-308-8

My Great Book Bookshelf

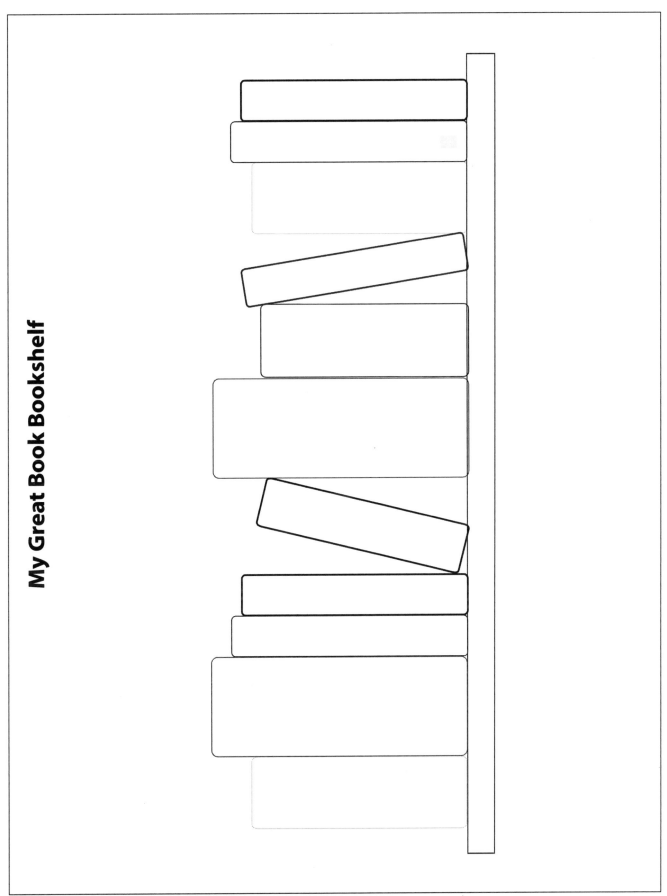

Pembroke Publishers © 2015 *This Is a Great Book!* by Larry Swartz and Shelley Stagg Peterson ISBN 978-1-55138-308-8

3

Independent Leisure Reading

"Reading ultimately belongs to readers, not schools, not school teachers."
— Donalyn Miller, *The Book Whisperer: Awakening the Inner Reader in Every Child*, page 171

If you love to read, then you likely know what leisure reading is. You probably look forward to those moments or hours when you can curl up among comfortable cushions or lounge in a chair on a sunny day, reading materials that you choose. Or, you may find ways to carve reading time into everyday activity, perhaps while waiting at a doctor's office or riding on a bus. Leisure reading is reading for one's own pleasure and purposes.

You read materials, whether they are print or electronic books, magazines or newspapers, website content or graphic novels, anticipating rewards. You may want to connect with a character you care about, find comfort and hope during a difficult time in your life, delight in getting into and out of exciting or troubling situations with a character, relish discovering something new about something, someone, or some place, or learn more on how to do something you have always wanted to do. There are as many reasons for reading as there are readers and materials for reading, as many reasons for reading as there are moments and places for reading. The important thing is that the reader makes the choices.

In the face of fiction reading in school, where reading for some can be anything but a pleasurable activity thanks to the removal of choice, what is required of students in terms of response, and the demands of standardized testing, we uphold the concept of "independent leisure reading." The International Literacy Association adopted this term in a position paper on leisure reading, and it points to the need for teachers to help students build a stamina for reading and understand or regain a sense that reading can be a pleasurable part of their lives.

In our classrooms, there is little good in teaching students to be readers, if they are not going to be readers for life. A serious, deliberate classroom ritual is required to make this happen. Indeed, in *Good Choice: Supporting Independent Reading and Response, K–6*, Tony Stead (2009, 4) advocates, "Independent reading needs to become an integral and focused component of a daily reading program, not simply an activity for early finishers or for settling down after lunch."

How Teacher Perceptions Affect Classroom Practice

In classrooms, independent leisure reading choices need to be made by the students, but teachers have a key role to play in promoting the activity. Effective teachers set a consistent daily time for independent leisure reading — 15 to 30 minutes, depending on the age of the students. They may also determine where students read, perhaps at their desks/tables, in a reading corner with cushions, or on the carpet. In that context, students choose reading materials according to their interests and reading abilities.

Many of the terms used to describe students' independent leisure reading (see the Wordle on the next page) reflect the primary goal of classroom leisure reading: to enhance students' motivation to read and self-confidence as readers. If students experience many rewards in their in-school leisure reading, it may well lead to their becoming lifelong readers.

But classroom leisure reading is also of more immediate value — there are recognized academic benefits to providing time for students to read materials of their choice, *especially* when they know that there will **not** be follow-up comprehension activities. For example, when they read a wide range of materials, students encounter new words and concepts. When the concepts are introduced within the context of a narrative, students gain a sense of how the words can be used — they are learning more than isolated definitions. Leisure reading is thus a natural forum for learning vocabulary and building general knowledge. Students also see how authors write dialogue, structure sentences, and develop characters. Essentially, as they read for pleasure, they note how authors model good writing, and the more they read, the greater the likelihood that they will begin to apply all these learnings in their own writing. Independent Reading time allows students to apply and practice reading strategies daily, enhancing their reading comprehension and achievement in reading.

Yet teachers have different perceptions about the place of Independent Reading time within their programs. Some teachers choose a specific time for independent leisure reading. Others can't seem to find time to "fit it all in." A further challenge is to have students respond to their independent leisure reading through writing or talk or the arts in order to gain further data for assessment. But Lisa Donohue has no doubts about the value of Independent Reading time. For the author of *Independent Reading: Inside the Box*, "setting students up for independent reading is crucial for establishing and maintaining an effective balanced reading program with an emphasis on small-group instruction" (2008, 10).

Donohue uses the term *independent reading*, but terminology pertaining to this kind of reading is as varied as the perceptions about it. The very terms teachers use say something about their approach to this aspect of the reading program. As part of reflecting on your independent reading program, consider the Wordle, the more traditional summary of terms, and the questions that follow.

In *Yellow Brick Roads: Shared and Guided Paths to Independent Reading, 4–12*, Janet Allen (2000, 98) writes that "the choices and attention and purpose during independent reading allow students to begin or continue the transition from teacher-directed reading in school to the kind of reading we do as adult readers."

What's in a name? What we have often called "leisure reading," a term which points to lifelong reading, goes by many different labels in the classroom. (This Wordle was devised by Randy Kirsh.)

Independent Reading	POWER (Providing Opportunities With Everyday Reading)
Recreational Reading	LTR (Love to Read)
Voluntary Reading	Self-Selected Reading
Spare Time Reading	Pleasure Reading
Free Reading	FVR (Free Voluntary Reading)
(DEAR) Drop Everything and Read	SQUIRT (Super Quiet Independent Reading Time)
Sustained Silent Reading	DIRT (Daily Independent Reading Time)

- Which term from the Wordle best describes your own independent leisure reading program?
- Besides the time factor, what are some challenges involved with incorporating leisure reading into your program?
- How important is it for students to track and respond to their independent reading?
- What elements do you think contribute to a significant independent reading program?

Some Issues Pertaining to Leisure Reading

Research surveying particular groups of readers reveals some alarming trends in the popularity of leisure reading beyond the classroom. We discuss these trends below.

Less Reading for Pleasure: Trend. Although the numbers of children who say they enjoy reading have been fairly stable, the numbers of young people who say they read regularly for pleasure have declined. See, for example, Clark's surveys for the U.K.'s National Literacy Trust, which surveyed young people ages 8 to 16 years old in November/December 2005 and again in 2012.

See "Boys, Novels, and Literacy" in Chapter 2.

Reading outside Class Time by Age. Younger students are more likely to say that they enjoy reading and that they read outside class time than older students. In a U.K. study, 14- to 16-year-old participants were twice as likely as 8- to 11-year-old students to say they never read outside class.

Love of Reading by Gender. On international surveys, such as Clark's 2012 survey for the U.K.'s National Literacy Trust, girls are more likely than boys to say that they enjoy reading, and girls engage in leisure reading more often than boys. This love of reading correlates with achievement on international literacy tests, as Grade 4 girls performed better than boys in all 34 countries where the Progress in International Reading Literacy Study (PIRLS) was administered. Recommendations to encourage boys to read include giving them choice in their reading materials, including digital and multimedia texts, as well as more action-oriented and humorous books. Inviting the children's male relatives, community celebrities, and other volunteers, as well as male teachers and school administrators, to read during independent leisure reading time provides male literacy models for boys, another important way to show that reading is more than a female activity (Booth 2002).

Making the Most of Classroom Leisure Reading Time

Decades ago, reading specialist Frank Smith concluded a presentation to a group of teachers by saying: "if literacy is going to live, it's going to live in our classrooms; if it's going to die, it's going to die in our classrooms." What we do from day to day to encourage independent readers depends on the texts we offer, the intensive and extensive opportunities for response we provide, and the enthusiasm we ourselves show for novels. An important goal teachers have for students is to foster positive attitudes towards reading as well as an openness to reading texts in a wide range of forms and on a variety of topics.

In any classroom there will be many students who look forward to leisure reading time, but some who do not. Many appreciate having time to read what *they* choose to read, catching up where they left off the previous day with a favorite character or discovering more about a topic of interest. Other students, we have observed, however, sort listlessly through reading materials, taking up much of their leisure reading time in a search for something to read. We see these students flipping through pages without engaging with the material. They are not realizing the benefits of leisure reading.

In the following pages, we present research-based practices that best support *all* students in making the most of classroom leisure reading time.

1. Make reading materials available for leisure reading

Creating a classroom library or reading center is a first step to promoting reading. Many teachers have gathered books of a wide range of genres, as well as magazines, newspapers, graphic novels, and perhaps comic books, to provide reading choices for students. If you have a wired classroom, you may also have ordered electronic books for students to read on laptops or tablets. Student-written stories and informational texts make a welcome addition to the classroom library. Students delight in reading something that peers have written and feel a great sense of pride when classmates read *their* writing.

"It is important for students to understand that there are many reasons a book is right for them at the time. It's not about levels. Often, there are more complex reasons to consider. If we can help students be in tune with their lives as readers, they will also be able to figure out when a book is not just right for them and why."
— Karen Szymusiak, Franki Sibberson, and Lisa Koch, *Beyond Leveled Books*, page 86

Bookstores can be inviting yet dangerous places for teachers, as we often emerge from them loaded with bags of books for our classroom libraries and a sizable credit card bill to pay at the end of the month. Stocking a classroom library does not have to involve bookstore purchases, however. You may want to borrow from the school library, rotate books monthly, and exchange books with colleagues. The free books that go along with Scholastic Book orders can also help to stock many classroom libraries.

The materials may be organized by genre and by reading difficulty. We advise against organizing by levels because often students can read materials beyond their assessed reading levels if they have background knowledge and experience about the topic and are keenly interested in it. Instead, you might organize shelves or bins using titles such as the following to show that some books are more challenging and some less challenging for most readers: (1) Speeding Ahead, (2) Going the Speed Limit, and (3) Taking Your Foot off the Gas.

2. Help students to select reading materials

Struggling readers often choose reading materials that are too difficult for them. Their resulting frustration prevents them from experiencing the benefits of leisure reading, and they become disengaged.

There are a number of ways for teachers to address this concern.

Teachers could, for example, promote familiarity with the locations of certain types of books within the building. They may want to co-plan this activity with the school librarian, if there is one, or make a field trip to the community's public library. The librarian could take children on a tour of the sections of the library that would most interest the age group of the students and read excerpts from books that she or he recommends.

"A Reading Interest Inventory" is useful for teachers when gathering books for classroom libraries and as a tool for students when selecting reading materials for leisure reading. See page 83.

Providing a demonstration on how to select books is helpful, as well. In the demonstration lesson, you might on take the role of a student in your class, acting as either an avid or a reluctant reader. You could discuss any or all of the following with the school librarian:

- types of reading materials that you have enjoyed reading in the past: favorite authors or series that you have read
- what you feel is a good book or magazine (e.g., lots of action, humor, characters you like, a topic that interests you — you can be specific about the topic)
- whether you want to continue reading the same types of materials or would use suggestions in "A Reading Interest Inventory" to try something new
- your responses after the librarian steers you towards similar types of books

For this latter aspect of the demonstration, you might read a page of a chosen book aloud or to yourself and then voice your thoughts, as if you were a student. Here are examples of what you might talk about:

- *summarizing what you got out of the first page*: "I can see that this book is going to be about _____. I always like [I don't really like] reading about . . ."
- *assessing ability to read the material without a struggle*: "I can understand everything/I can't understand what the author is talking about here . . ."
- *assessing whether you would enjoy reading the text*: "I want to keep reading about . . . The author writes in a way that makes me want to read more." "This is a really boring start. Because I like the topic, I'll try another page or two, but after that, I'm moving on to another book."

The Persuasiveness of Peer Recommendations

"Enthusiastic recommendations from a student peer can make the new more approachable. Such recommendations can occur in conversation or be posted online in forums such as Just Read It. Encourage students to engage in this kind of peer sharing, both informally and through student-led book talks and online posts.

"Students often recommend Rick Riordan's *The Lightning Thief*, also a good example of a novel that has subsequently been made into a graphic novel and a film, something that provides additional points of access. This novel, along with The Secret Series by Pseudonymous Bosch and *11 Birthdays* by Wendy Mass, are popular student recommendations and are also the first of a set. As such, they can spur students on to immediate further reading. This extended reading is particularly valuable, fostering the habit of reading longer, richer books."
— Mary Catherine Doyle, teacher-librarian

"Any book that helps a child to form a habit of reading, to make reading one of his deep and continuing needs is good for him."
— Maya Angelou, poet laureate

You and the librarian could then summarize what students can do when selecting reading materials.

In addition to providing a formal library visit or demonstration, teachers seeking to help students choose books are wise to engage in promotional practices, such as these:

- Make available novels that vary by topic, author, and level of difficulty, and give students several novels from which to choose.
- Be aware of the students' interests and needs, talking to the students about their reading, and surveying students to find current favorites.
- Advertise and promote various titles on classroom and school bulletin boards, and in newsletters sent or e-mailed home to parents and guardians — book fair notices can help parents choose and buy books for their children. Encourage students to share their opinions of books with their peers, and pass on comments of librarians and reviewers to them.
- Do your best to display books in an inviting way. We recommend making book covers visible to students who are choosing books for their independent leisure reading.
- Read aloud part or all of a novel, and recommend other books on the same theme or by the same author if students show interest.

Remember, though, that choice belongs to the student. When students choose books, they should be able to make personal choices from the classroom collection and to seek advice from peers, as well as from adults who know their abilities and interests and can identify suitable novels for them to read. They will do best reading books by an author or on a theme that appeals to them. They should be free to abandon any book they are not enjoying and **not** have to defend their tastes. Having them keep a log of books read is a good idea — for each book, students could note the title and author's name, as well as a few details about the story to remind them about the characters and plot.

How to Choose a Book: Summary for Students

1. Go to a section of the library that has the types of materials you have enjoyed reading in the past or to a section that has a new type of material you want to try. The "Reading Interest Inventory" that your teacher may give you makes some suggestions about new materials.
2. Think about what you like in the kind of text you want to read.
3. Using your criteria for what you like, select something to read.
4. Read the first page to yourself, and do any or all of the following. Summarize what you got out of the first page, and assess whether you like reading about the topic. Consider whether you can read the text without too much difficulty. Assess whether the author writes in a style likely to keep you interested.

---

3. Create an engaging environment for reading

Make independent leisure reading time a regularly scheduled part of the school day, so that students can anticipate having time to read independently and reading becomes a habit for them. Although not essential that the teacher read during this time, remember that modeling reading behavior benefits children. Students' reading time can be scheduled at any time that makes sense for the classroom timetable.

Before or after the independent leisure reading time, take an opportunity to talk about books that you have read, read about, or acquired for the class. When a teacher talks about his or her own leisure reading, it serves to model the importance of the practice. It may also help students make their book choices.

Children can read at their desks or at tables. On a rotating basis, they might also be allowed to read among pillows or sofas, or in whatever special setup there may be in the classroom library area.

For young children, you can circumvent avoidance behaviors that may occur during reading time through pre-emptive classroom management. As an example, bathroom breaks could be arranged before independent reading begins.

Bear in mind that leisure reading time in primary grades may not be silent reading time. Many young children find it helpful to vocalize while reading.

Students should not be discouraged from doing so and, indeed, could be paired up with a peer to read quietly aloud during leisure reading time.

Remember, too, that when you as a teacher talk about a children's book, young adult book, magazine, graphic novel, or comic you have enjoyed, students will find your excitement contagious. You will not only be promoting the particular text you are talking about, but even if your students do not choose to read your recommended book, you will be modeling a love of reading that endures throughout life.

4. Monitor students' reading

The following assessment line masters can be used to help monitor students' reading:
- Reading Observation Checklist
- Self-Assessment: Reflecting on Your Novel Reading
- Reading Observation Checklist
These appear on appendix pages 130, 131, and 132.

Reading inventories provide a record of the interests and tastes of readers. They also provide a tool to monitor the students' reading interests at different times of the year. Students can self-monitor their reading by keeping a record of the titles they have read and listing the genres associated with these titles.

Title	Author	Type of Book*	Date Completed

Observing the students' behaviors is important to determine how motivated and engaged they are as they read.

5. Follow up with activities and talk about books to deepen students' engagement

A number of activities at the end of this chapter offer ways for students to reflect on their leisure reading.

Elementary teachers in Sault Ste. Marie, Ontario, found that when their students talked with a peer about what they had read during leisure reading time, all students' engagement with books increased, and they made the most of leisure reading time. Researchers have found that these after-reading discussions helped English Language Learners with their overall language learning, too, because they had an authentic conversation in a low-threat environment (Carrison and Ernst-Slavit 2005; Krashen 2011).

---

*Examples of "Type of Book" include adventure, mystery, realistic fiction, and fantasy.

The Secret Ingredient

by Fatma Faraj

Fatma Faraj is a children's literature enthusiast and teacher-librarian.

When people find out what I do for a living, they automatically say: "You must read a lot!" Of course, I do. Reading a lot doesn't always mean reading all the best books in publishing. Not every book can be the best book, but there are a lot of great books. And there are a lot of readers, especially a lot of *different* readers. A good book for one person may be a great book for someone else.

As a junior school teacher-librarian, I find that one of the greatest moments is when I hand a book to a student who comes back a few days later and says: "That was a great book!" This doesn't happen every time, but I have devised a list of ingredients to help create the best recipe for sharing a great book. To understand how this recipe works, one needs to understand the recipe it takes for me find my next great read.

Here's what I do: I scroll through my social media platforms — Twitter, Facebook, Pinterest, and favorite blogs — to see where the buzz is online. If I have more time, I wander through classrooms and talk to colleagues, or I may stop at a bookstore on the way home and cruise the bookshelves. Sometimes, books come to me via a text from a friend who has read a great book. Last, but not least, I love workshops and presentations. I love to hear how people find the magic in a book that makes it great. There are times when I hear about a book that I may have overlooked because I didn't stay with it long enough — I needed someone to share it with me again. Taking this all into account, I decided to think about how students interact with me in the library and how I help guide them to a great book.

Authors: Rock Stars of the Reading World

Teacher-librarians know that authors are the readers' version of a rock star. Students will follow an author and find their books on the shelves. One way to get the students into the library and to take out a book is to let them know that their favorite author has a new book (and we have it). Invite a student to be the first from the school to read the book. When you hand the student the book, there is a mini-celebration, and for a minute you are the rock star, but then the student starts to gush about the author's other titles, reminding you that you are just the messenger and the author is the star.

Every day can't be a rock concert in the library. Author visits are few and far between based on publication dates and costs to the library, and writing a book takes time. So, how do I bring the same element to the library plus add what works with me to the mix? I went back to the test kitchen to figure out how I can bring rock star fun to the library. I needed to create a new recipe, with a dash of one special ingredient. Just like Goldilocks when she's in the house of the three bears, I have come up with the "just right" ingredients to hand my students the next best read.

Know Your Students' Tastes

Take time and get to know your students. I know it's hard to learn everyone's name and what they like, but recognizing a student by a book is an amazing way to make connections. Many times, I see the book and the student at the same time. I know, if a new book has been published, which student will ask for it first. That's the first part of knowing your students' tastes. Watch where they go in the library: is it to graphic novels, non-fiction, chapter books, series, or picture books? This is where I have developed a passion for all types of books. When I was a child, I would always head to the fiction spinners in the library. The only time you would catch me in non-fiction would be because I had a project to complete. As literacy teachers, we are getting better every day at recognizing the different types of texts available to students. Students appreciate when you have a new book on the latest skateboarding tricks or on how to mummify a body in ancient Egypt.

Share the Books in a Creative Display

I was never the best teacher when it came to decorating bulletin boards. However, as a teacher-librarian and user of Twitter I have changed how I use my display areas. When trolling for ideas, you will see that many libraries around the world have amazing displays. This year, for example, we covered book covers with blank paper so the reader couldn't see the author name or book title. The only text on the blank paper was the first line of the book. Students, teachers, and parents had fun guessing the titles and were happy to sign out the books, taking the paper off them as if the books were gifts.

One student who loved looking at the displays took it upon herself to create a sign and display some of her favorite series of books. Other teachers got involved in this student's work and wanted their favorite series to be on display, too. A brother of one of my students was looking at the display and was happy to see some of his favorite books there. He was encouraging his sister to sign out some of them. Book displays inspire conversation and can encourage others to share the next great book.

Walk the Shelves with the Students

When students come into the library and I don't have a class, I like to join them in their walk along the shelves. Students shouldn't feel like they always need to go to the computer to find a book. If they are looking for a specific title, it makes sense to see if the book is available, but some of the greatest books I have ever read I found by "walking the shelves."

Take time and find a book by the color of the spine or the font of the title. Judge a book by its cover and discover! The coolest part about walking the shelves with students is that I am reminded of books I loved at certain times in my life. I still get excited when I see my favorite female sleuth, or my favorite family, or that random title that someone recommended to me. The students want to know that it is okay to judge a book by its cover and that sometimes the hidden books — the ones that don't always make it to the displays — are the greatest books.

Find Reading Allies

Sometimes, the ingredient isn't about what I think about a book, it's what students' friends think about the book that matters. Every year, as I get to know the students and their reading tastes, I target a specific reader. I may invite that child to peruse the special shelf of new books in the office (Hot off the Presses!). Students love to be the first reader of a book new to the library, something I learned from my childhood librarians, who would magically pull a book from underneath their desk or their office shelf and say, "I think you'll like this." Other things would be put aside, as I went home to read this special gift of a book. I couldn't wait to go back to the librarian to let her know that I had read the book and she could now share it with others.

Now, it's not only the librarian with whom the students are sharing the book — students start talking about the book before it's returned to the library. Some great books sign themselves out to the students because of the first hand off. My allies in reading keep the book in the hands of other readers, and it becomes a legend in its own right.

Read and Share — the Secret Ingredient

That's the secret. It seems so simple, but it's the greatest gift of sharing the greatest book in the library. Read the book and share your love of the book with the students. Students want to know that you know the characters and the situations in the book.

When I read a book that I know I *have* to share, I find the classroom teacher and say, "I have a book I would like to share with your class!" Or if the students are visiting the library for a lesson, I may sneak in a book talk, where I promote books that I really like and that I know many students have enjoyed.

Sharing the news of the next great book is like sharing a secret. Students and teachers lean forward in their seats and want to be the first one to borrow the book. When a book becomes such a word-of-mouth sensation, it is my job to purchase multiple copies. Again, thinking of all types of readers, I will research if the book is available in audiobook format or other e-text compatibilities. It is important that the text is accessible for all.

Recently, one of my students was reading through the Harry Potter series. She knew I had read the series and was excited to share her adventures at Hogwarts. I bumped into her one morning on the walk to school and she wasn't very talkative. (This was odd, as she was a member of my book club and loved to share what she was reading.) We were almost at the school when she turned to me and recounted the events that occurred in the book she had read during her breakfast. She had me so excited, even though I had read the book before, I had to revisit the book when I arrived in the library. Read and share — it's a mutual event. The ingredient doesn't always come from the teacher-librarian. It can come from the student.

The gift of sharing the next great book can be as simple as a 30-second conversation in the hallway or holding up a book as students walk by the library. It's important to know your community of readers. Students know that I am always looking for the next best book and that I am always willing to share. The books are way too delicious to keep to myself.

Give a Book, Take a Book: Promoting Reading in the Community

In 2009, retired Wisconsin teacher Todd Bol began Little Free Library (Little FreeLibrary.org), a non-profit organization to further promote a love of reading. As a result, rather small, decorated bookshelves, usually with a glass door, have popped up in North American and European communities — more than 20,000 around the world — to provide a gathering place where anyone can stop by, select one or two books, and bring back another to share. These book-filled boxes are conversation starters, encouraging passersby to "take a book or leave a book." Besides the curiosity factor (what's on display today?), neighbors begin to know one another as they peruse collections displayed on front lawns, thus forging personal connections, connecting readers to books, and even inspiring book talk between givers and takers.

Many of the Little Free Library books are geared towards children, where students can donate books, take a book to keep, or read and return books that can be passed on to others — this project could be an exciting one for students to undertake in their own communities.

Caution: The program has not been without detractors. Some claim that the libraries are in violation of city codes, that permits have not been acquired to erect public bookshelves, or that the birdhouse-like libraries may cause some obstructions.

Book Pass: Finding the Right Book

by Joan O'Callaghan

Joan O'Callaghan is a literacy instructor at the Ontario Institute for Studies in Education, University of Toronto.

I am always open to finding ways to promote a love a reading with students. While reading a journal a few years ago, I came across a strategy called Book Pass that several teachers found to be successful for inspiring independent leisure reading. I decided to give it a try, and it has personally become a favorite way to help readers choose the book that best suits their interests, needs, and tastes.

I arrive in the classroom, with a range of novels that I have acquired from my own book collection, from colleagues, and from the school library. The novels can include a variety of genres. Alternatively, the titles can have a connection by theme, genre, or author. (On one occasion, I had a collection of novels by Gary Paulsen and presented *Hatchet*, *The Island*, *Dogsong*, *Tracker*, and other Paulsen books, mostly on the theme of survival, to the students.)

Books are randomly distributed to students, who are instructed to read the book they have received for three minutes. If a book grabs a student, he or she can opt out of the rotation and keep reading that book. If someone doesn't favor the book, it is passed to someone nearby. Students are then given another three-minute time period to meet a new book. The passing of books continues until most students have found a book that they are unwilling to relinquish until they have finished reading it.

I am pleased with the activity since the students are responsible for making their own choices. Students are happy because they are given choice. Following the book choosing, we become a community of readers, where each student can share his or her enthusiasms and responses to the novels. Book Pass allows me to find the right book for the right reader. It ignites an authentic independent reading component of my novel program.

Young Readers Exercising Choice

When selecting novels for students' leisure reading, for read-alouds, and for classroom activities, teachers can feel confident that books on the young readers' choice lists will be engaging for their students. These lists contain books that thousands of children have chosen as their favorites from a selection of dozens and, in some cases, hundreds of titles. Numerous books are selected for the awards each year, so there is a good chance that teachers will find titles on these lists that will interest all students in their classes. The book lists can be found readily on websites: see, for example, www.bookcentre.ca/awards/canadian_awards_index, which lists titles of the Canadian Children's Award Index of the Canadian Children's Book Centre.

Students' participation in the selection process is invaluable for enhancing their motivation to read and for developing strong identities as readers, as students' opinions of the books they read are valued by children and adults within and beyond the school. Participation in the selection process also creates a community of readers within the classroom and within the school, as children make recommendations to peers about books they have read, perhaps posting their reviews of the books on a classroom or school blog or bulletin board.

Among the awards are the Children's Choice Book Awards, a joint project of the International Literacy Association and the Children's Book Council recognizing books published in the United States — this program is international in scope. Other awards include the Pacific Northwest Library Association Young Readers

Choice Award, a regional award where books are selected by students in Grades 4 to 12 living in Alberta, British Columbia, Alaska, Idaho, Montana, Oregon, and Washington; and awards for books published in Canada, such as the following:

- Hackmatack Children's Choice Book Award — Atlantic provinces (books selected by children in Grades 4 to 6)
- Manitoba Young Readers' Choice Award (books selected by children in Grades 5 to 8)
- Diamond Willow Award — Saskatchewan (books selected by children in Grades 4 to 8)
- Rocky Mountain Award — Alberta (books selected by children in Grades 4 to 7)
- Golden Eagle Children's Choice Award — southern Alberta (books selected by children in Grades 4 to 7)

A Flourishing Awards Program with National Impact

The Forest of Reading program run by the Ontario Library Association (OLA) has become a successful venture that invigorates reading across Canada. The underlying philosophy of the initiative, first established in 1994, is to encourage, promote, and support Canadian books for readers, which it most certainly does. Moreover, Forest of Reading provides teachers, teacher-librarians, library staff, and parents with a meaningful tool for improving literacy in schools and libraries.

Forest of Reading has become the largest recreational reading program in Canada. The unique feature of the program is that students are allowed to make their own choices about reading by voting for their favorite books. It is made up of eight programs geared towards readers in Kindergarten to Grade 12. There are non-fiction and fiction titles in each category. Specific to the reading of novels, titles are chosen for the following:

- Silver Birch, for students in Grades 3 to 6
- Red Maple, for students in Grades 6 to 8
- White Pine, for high-school students

By reading five titles in a given category, students are given the opportunity to determine a winning author. Teacher-librarian Karen Upper points out that "there is a certain competitive spirit among many students, motivating them to become avid readers. A desire to surpass their peers creates a ripple effect. Students of all reading tastes and levels read voraciously in a variety of genres that they would normally bypass."

Nominated books for any category are first read, scrutinized, and discussed by a team of volunteer adult readers. These pre-selected lists are made available to students, usually within the school library. Many teachers comment how reluctant readers are excited to select books from the competitive list and often want more books by the author on a similar theme, thus inviting students to go deeper into the forest of reading.

Helpful U.S. Websites Featuring Children's Recommendations

Children's Choices Reading List: American children from Kindergarten to Grade 6 choose from a selection of approximately 500 books each year their favorite books to create the Children's Choices Reading List. This program is co-sponsored by the International Literacy Association and the Children's Book Center. Annotated lists of these books can be found at http://literacyworldwide. org/get-resources/reading-lists/childrens-choices-reading-list.

Young Adults' Choices Reading List: American young adults from Grades 7 to 12 choose their favorite books each year to create this list. Annotated lists of these books can be found at http://literacyworldwide.org/get-resources/reading-lists/young-adults-choices-reading-list.

International Educators' Recommendations

Whether they be teachers or librarians, adults, too, vote to identify books that are likely to attract young people as readers.

United States: Sponsored by the International Literacy Association, the Teachers' Choices Reading List program invites American teachers to select new books that engage their students. Annotated lists of the books, organized by year, can be found at http://literacyworldwide.org/get-resources/reading-lists/teachers-choices-reading-list.

On the New York Public Library website is 100 Great Children's Books: 100 Years, an annotated list, organized alphabetically, of books that children's librarians at the New York Public Library say are "still flying off our shelves." See http://www.nypl.org/childrens100.

United Kingdom: Each year, the U.K. BookTrust publishes *The Book Trust Best Book Guide*. Find links for the guides, organized in four age groups (from birth to age 14 and beyond) at http://www.booktrust.org.uk/books/children/best-book-guide/.

In 2013, the BookTrust children's literature experts created the 100 Best Books for Children published in the last 100 years. See http://www.booktrust.org.uk/programmes/primary/childrens-book-week/100-best-books/.

New Zealand: The New Zealand Post Children's Choice Award list introduces books that children and young adults love to read and that are published in New Zealand. The winning books are identified on the Christchurch City Libraries website, but there are no annotations. See http://christchurchcitylibraries.com/Kids/LiteraryPrizes/NZPost/Choice.

FEATURE

Have I Got a Book for You!

by Wendy Mason

Wendy Mason, a bookseller for more than 15 years, has been a juror for the TD Canadian Children's Literature Awards.

I am a passionate bookseller, and my greatest joy emanates from recommending and then selling a book that resonates with the reader's interests. Parents, kids, grandparents, and teachers come to my department for suggestions. It's a timely process that involves asking questions, being a good listener, and then keeping up-to-date on current books that will fulfill the reader/buyer request. Many parents know only the popular titles and that's always okay with me because I know that I can move from there. Teachers come with curriculum book needs. Grandparents come wanting suggestions.

What I try to do is introduce *other* books that might move the reader to a different level without compromising the reader's interests. I promote Canadian first since we have so many talented authors and illustrators whose work is often unread or unseen, but that doesn't preclude me from recommending authors from countries around the world. Deciding what to recommend boils down to the intimate conversation between the reader, the buyer, and me, and what is best to keep a book in a young person's hands.

The clientele I serve can be broken down into adults (including teachers), adults accompanied by kids, and kids only, with whom I interact directly. Each kind of client requires a different approach and a different role for me. Some parents rely on my role as an expert bookseller to suggest books for their children, while others may have different opinions about what they want to buy for their children. I've had parents who say they want only books that are "pure in content." Young readers roll their eyes, and I know that they want the freedom to select from the variety of offerings I place in their hands. When young people approach me in the bookstore, they often say they want something new and different — and less boring — than the books they are assigned to read in school.

A Compass, a Travel Guide, a Cheerleader

At times, I am a compass, just pointing kids in the direction of popular books that sit on the many shelves of series books appropriate for their age group. As students encounter and develop their reading habits with novels, I find that kids read what their friends are reading. The cash register tells us so.

Often, I am curious about what the child is currently reading so that I can make further recommendations to satisfy the reader's tastes and needs. In this way, I serve as a travel guide to genres, authors, and titles that the child can, I hope, connect to. I have great success recommending books by Eric Walters due to the diversity of topics and interest levels his work reflects. Susan Nielsen, Gordon Korman, and Deborah Ellis are other Canadian authors who appeal to many young readers.

I also enjoy being a cheerleader for titles that I feel are great because I myself have enjoyed reading them and am, therefore, keen to pass on recommendations to readers open to suggestions.

As a person there in the store to sell books, I, of course, feel satisfaction when the kids, parents, grandparents, and teachers come to visit the department once again and ask me for more recommendations. When that happens, I know that my suggestions have worked and that I have been a part of keeping a child reading, a grandparent sharing, or a teacher introducing the pleasure of the "right" book with a class.

Ultimately, my job is to "sell" books, but make no mistake: this has nothing to do with the cash register. For me, it's a matter of offering novels to readers who might not choose them on their own. Being a compass, a travel guide, or a cheerleader, I enjoy the thrill of cultivating readers and connecting books to young readers. It's exciting to hear the words "This is a great book!"

Yes, this is a great job!

Bookseller's Choice

Wendy Mason recommends these titles for young people ages 10 to 14:

Cut Off by Jamie Bastedo
Living Outside the Lines by Lesley Choyce
Under the Moon by Deborah Kerbel
Masterminds by Gordon Korman
Rain, Reign by Ann M. Martin
We're All Made of Molecules by Susin Nielsen
Wonder by R. J. Palacio
Unlikely Hero of Room 13B by Teresa Toten
The Boy in the Dress by David Walliams
Walking Home by Eric Walters

Novels and Me

Interview with Zachary Hastie

In the following interview, Zachary Hastie, a student in Grade 6, answers questions about his novel reading. Zachary talks about his fondness for reading series books and shares his views of reading inside and outside school

1.   What are your first memories of reading novels?

When I was younger I still wanted to read picture books, but one day I decided it was time to start *really* reading. I remember when I got my first novel, which was the first book in the Magic Tree House series. I thought that if I didn't like the book, it was OK because maybe it just wasn't a good novel for me. So I read a chapter to see, but the chapters were only a few pages. So I thought maybe I should read another chapter, but what I didn't realize is that I was actually hooked and without a thought, I finished it.

2.   How do you think you developed an interest in reading novels?

After I finished that first book, I wanted to read more. I was given a box set of Magic Tree House books and I knew I wanted to get through the series. The reasons why I liked this book is because it has some pictures which reminded me of picture books and also helped me to visualize better. Another reason is because it had magic. After I finished the Magic Tree House books, I thought, what else has magic in it? My older brother liked reading Harry Potter, which was about magic. So I started reading it. It was interesting but long. Maybe a bit too long. If my brother could read it, so could I. I started with my mom reading the books to me. My brother gave me some of the other novels he enjoyed. I really liked the Animorphs series and Captain Underpants. Then I gradually started reading more and more advanced novels (longer).

3.   What series do you particularly enjoy reading now? What is it about the series that you enjoy?

Right now I'm in the middle of one of the Goosebumps books. What I like about this [book] is that it's a horror book. Really R. L. Stine books are not too scary and don't give me nightmares. Another reason I like Goosebumps books is that I still like short novels so I can finish them quickly and move on to the next book in the series. Since I own a lot of Goosebumps books, the adventures will go on for a long time. Another series that I enjoy is the Skeleton Creek series. There is a mystery in each of the books, and the mystery just keeps growing. I also like the author's style of writing a journal from the main character's point of view. It made mystery adventure a bit more realistic.

4.   What do you think makes a book a great book?

I think what makes a book great is that the book has a plot that keeps you going. I can sort of tell at the beginning of the book that the plot will lead to something great. It should catch your attention right away. The author shouldn't just make you feel like you're reading the book but actually inside the book as the characters, living the book. The book also has to match the genre that the reader likes to read. For me it would be fantasy, adventure, horror, and mystery. I imagine myself in those worlds, and even if they are scary or magical, I know it's just a book, but a *great* book 'cause I imagine myself in those worlds.

5. *What is a book that you particularly enjoyed reading this year in school? What activity did you enjoy working on that helped you respond to the novel?*

In school there were two different activities. I liked the book *Wonder*. While my teacher read the book to us we got to draw, which helped me concentrate on the book better and visualize. We had some good discussions about Auggie, and I often thought about what would happen if Auggie went to our school.

We also got to read a book of our choice and write a connection. I think the connection project was good because you could choose your book, and I liked doing connections because it wasn't easy and I had to think deeper about my book and what it meant to me.

6. *How is reading novels in school different than reading novels outside of school?*

I like when the teacher reads aloud. We also worked in groups and did activities to help us think about the book. I liked that the teacher let us choose our books to then form our groups. In groups we read a part of a book at home, did an activity that we were assigned by our group, brought it back to school, showed our work to the group, and repeated. Outside of school, I can read whatever I want whenever I want instead of having to read the book at home, finishing a certain part, and completing an activity by the next day. The best time for me is the summer time.

7. *Who do you think has helped you become a better reader?*

My mother: She took me to the library every other week since I was a little kid.

My brother: He is three years older than me and loves to read. Lots. I sometimes like the books he's reading, but I don't always want to read what he liked (Percy Jackson series).

My friends: I like to read what they're reading. They like to read what I'm reading.

My teacher: He helps me to think about books in better ways.

My uncle: He takes me to bookstores to buy books. He lets me choose whatever I want.

8. *Besides novels, what other things do you like to read?*

Besides novels I like to read comics. I really like the TMNT (Teenage Mutant Ninja Turtles), and Sonic comics. For TMNT I collect all of the new series; for Sonic comics I collect only the Sonic Universe comics. Besides comics and novels I read Manga, a Japanese comic book in a big book form. Each book has about eight chapters in it. I like to read the One Piece Manga.

9. *Do you think boys read different books than girls?*

I think boys read different types of books than girls depending on the age. I think when people get older, they end up reading the same books as each other because my friends love books about fantasy and magic. I also see that girls like that kind of book. At the beginning of the school year, we started with a survey about different people's interests. Everyone has to ask everyone a question and record it. We completed a double bar graph to compare boys' and girls' book interests. Most of the options were even. I don't think that's true every age. If you ask my two little cousins that are girls, they love *Frozen*, and I know that a lot of people love *Frozen*. But some little boys don't like *Frozen*. Which goes into two different groups. This could lead into what type of books each gender likes more: the girls more for princesses, and the boys more for fighting and action.

*10. I really really liked the following novel . . . [fill in the blank]. Here is something I
learned about life by reading this novel.*

I really really liked the novel *Skeleton Creek* by Patrick Carman. His style of writing and putting you inside the adventure to help solve the mystery makes you feel like you're part of the story. The author puts in codes to watch a video at a website. The videos seem like they have actually happened. Something I learned about life while reading this book is, you can't always rely on the Internet for answers; the best way to find answers or information is to ask people, observing what is around you, or reading other books that can give you more information. Which makes you want to read more and more books . . .

Helping Students Reflect on Their Leisure Reading: Activities

When students first think about leisure reading, they might consider the books in their lives. In truth, readers read all kinds of things, for all kinds of reasons (from magazines and newspapers to website pages and e-mails). Reading for pleasure is not just about entering the world of fiction. As David Booth argues, all the reading anyone does should be "for pleasure." When readers engage with texts, bringing meaning, finding information, or wandering inside and outside a narrative, they should be having a pleasurable experience.

Activity 3-1: A Personal Inventory

You may want to have students complete this survey at the beginning of the year and then again after engaging in much independent reading inside and outside the classroom. Alternatively, they could work with "Reading Interest Inventory," which is on page 83.

To help students understand themselves as readers, it's important for them to think about what they read, how they read, and how often they read. Everyone has different attitudes, feelings, and interests related to reading. "My Leisure Reading Inventory" (page 82) can be used to help students reflect on the significance of leisure reading in their lives and become more metacognitively aware of their reading preferences and habits. After they complete the inventory on their own, they can meet in small groups, comparing responses and attitudes. When they talk with others about their responses to the prompts, students' perceptions of possibilities for their own reading can be expanded.

Activity 3-2: Tracking Independent Reading

This activity provides students with an opportunity to research their reading habits. Before students do the activity, talk with them about using the information they will gather to help them set goals for their reading patterns. Have students prepare the following chart and then track their reading behaviors for a 24-hour period (or for one school day).

What I Read	Amount of Time	Independent Choice	Inside School	Outside School

Extension: As a follow-up to this activity, students can analyze the data by answering these questions.

- What are your strengths as an independent reader?
- What are some patterns you see in your reading behaviors?
- What goals might you set to improve your independent reading practice?

Activity 3-3: Having a Conversation on Paper

This activity invites students to record reactions about a topic or issue and to consider the views of others. By sharing their responses with one or two peers, students can discover whether their opinions on independent leisure reading are similar or different. They can have a "conversation" on paper.

1. Students choose one of the statements below.
   - I don't have time to read and that's the way it is.
   - I enjoy reading only if I can choose what I read.
   - The book industry is dying.
   - I don't like to read . . . [fill in the blank]
   - Owning your own books is too expensive.
2. On a piece of paper, students write one or two statements that express an opinion in response.
3. Students exchange papers with a classmate. Partners read what has been written and respond by writing one or two sentences.
4. Papers continue to be passed back and forth, as if the students are having a conversation.

Activity 3-4: Independent's Day

Prompt students to organize a day devoted to independent reading. The celebration could be for a single class or spread out to a grade division or perhaps the whole school.

To begin, suggest that a set time be set aside for independent reading; then, students might do any of the following:

- Document the total number of minutes dedicated to independent reading in the class.
- Survey the class to find out who is reading fiction and who is reading nonfiction. Create a graph to record results.
- Create a bibliography of items read. Perhaps it might be an annotated bibliography, where each person contributes an item to the list.
- Create a video recording of interviews of volunteers sharing their independent reading experiences.

My Leisure Reading Inventory

1. What are some thing(s) you particularly like to read?

    _____

2. What is your favorite place to read?

    _____

3. What is your favorite time of day to read?

    _____

4. Name a book that is important to you.

    _____

5. Do you have a bookshelf or rack of your own? If yes, about how many books do you own?

    _____

6. If you read books regularly, what do you like about reading? Or, if you don't read books on a regular basis, why not?

    _____

7. What advice would you give to a teacher about including leisure reading in the program?

    _____

8. How is "school reading" different or the same than reading outside school?

    _____

9. How much time in a typical day do you estimate you spend with leisure reading?
    (a) Less than 30 minutes   (b) between 30 and 60 minutes   (c) over 60 minutes

10. What kind of reading do you do that you consider to be leisure reading?

    _____

11. Why is leisure reading important?

    _____

12. List the titles you have read as part of your leisure reading in the past week.

    _____

    _____

    _____

Reading Interest Inventory

The following inventory is designed for you to consider the types of books you like to read and the ones you might want to read. By checking the appropriate column (√), you will gain a thorough picture of your reading interests. When you select books for independent leisure reading, you may want to bring this inventory with you to remind you of types of reading materials you might choose. I will make a copy of this to help me make selections for our classroom library.

Types of Reading Materials	Often read	Sometimes read	Don't read but want to	Don't read and don't want to
Adventure stories				
Sports stories				
Mysteries				
Historical stories				
Vampire/horror stories				
Comic books				
Graphic novels				
Realistic stories				
Humorous stories				
Fantasy stories				
Science-fiction stories				
Picture books				
Non-fiction books about animals				
Non-fiction books about technology				
Non-fiction books about space				
Non-fiction books about people				
Non-fiction books about countries				
Non-fiction books about sports				
Non-fiction about _____ [fill in your choice]				
Poetry				
Magazines about sports				
Magazines about movies/TV stars				
Magazines about animals				
Magazines about technology				
Magazines about world events				
Magazines about _____ [fill in your choice]				
Newspapers				

Pembroke Publishers © 2015 *This Is a Great Book!* by Larry Swartz and Shelley Stagg Peterson ISBN 978-1-55138-308-8

4

Responding to Novels

"If books could have more, give more, be more, show more, they would still need readers, who bring to them sound and smell and all the rest that can't be in books."
— Gary Paulsen, from *The Winter Room*, page 3

How students respond to what they read can be as important as what they read. Response activities can take the form of discussion, writing, drama, or art. Students can talk about a text, write about ideas sparked by the novel, read dialogue aloud, model play-dough sculptures or create three-dimensional art, role-play characters and events, illustrate, and read other novels by the same author. When they express their personal responses to literature and other forms of texts freely, they demonstrate their growth as literature learners.

Opening Up the Text

A sampling of 12 detailed response activities appears at the end of this chapter. There are also ideas outlined under response mode headings pertaining to visual arts, drama, and media and technology.

Reading for Reading's Sake

Remember: You do not always have to ask for an external response. On occasion, the reading of a novel is a complete experience in itself. Students may call upon it later, but not be required to respond right away. Usually, though, in the context of a literacy program, students should do something with what they have read.

Response activities allow readers to open up the text for interpretation and reflection — to make sense of the novel they have read. By responding in a format that suits their learning style, students can consider the experience of reading and expand or modify their understanding. Response activities encourage readers to voice viewpoints and opinions and to share and compare these responses with the viewpoints and opinions of others. With careful intervention on the teacher's part, collaborative responses can extend each reader's personal response and help generate a wider and more thoughtful appreciation of the book.

Helping students go beyond the text requires techniques that relate the ideas and concepts in the text to the students' experiences and that tap fundamental memories and connections brought forth by the intensity of the reading experience. In the classroom, we can promote and develop the students' responses by opening up the text for discussion and encouraging students to express their ideas and opinions: opinions that are relevant to, but not necessarily identical to those in the novel.

Response activities that follow students' reading are, indeed, intended to extend and enrich their print experiences — they should not take the place of reading. Time spent selecting, planning, and completing activities provides real reasons for students to make a close reading of the text, and that can lead to significant dialogue. The teacher helps students decide what modes of response are appropriate and how they want to respond (individually, with a partner, or as part of a group). The students then each choose a response mode that will help them direct their own learning.

A sense of trust during response time allows students to revisit and reflect on the novel reading experience and to modify their understanding. When students reveal their responses with others (and this can happen best through group book talk), they can simultaneously check their own understandings and help one another to find new meanings. In *Tell Me*, author Aidan Chambers points out that sharing with others allows us to rub our ideas and opinions against those of other members of the group, and can often lead us together to insights we might never have discovered alone.

As students articulate their interpretations and learn from others' different viewpoints, knowledge, and experience, they also begin to appreciate the complexities of a good novel. They may notice how appropriate and effective particular words and expressions are. When students respond to some of the novels they have read, they will start to explore the more traditional elements of literature: plot, characterization, setting, theme, style, and opinion. For the most part, these concepts are brought up by the students in their own questioning or inquiry. When such terms of reference are useful, they can be explained. The knowledge about novels thus grows from need and context.

Response Activity Goals

It is important that we find a balance between promoting and encouraging reading and assigning activities that require response in order to help deepen students' comprehension. Of course, we want to do both. The following list is intended to help teachers consider what they want students to achieve through engaging in response activities:

- Students will read carefully.
- Students will extend their knowledge.
- Students will make and share connections.
- Students will elaborate on first understandings.
- Students will discover new patterns of thought.
- Students with interact with others.

Approaches to Response

Teachers' choice of instruction for response will vary from classroom to classroom. Each teacher develops a belief and a theory about how he or she feels literature needs to be taught, and this theory emerges from background experiences as a student, in coursework the teacher has taken, in professional reading, and from reflective practice. Many novel guides are available from publishers or online to accompany novels, and teachers draw questions and activities from such sources. Other teachers may set up Literature Circles, where students meet in groups to discuss books. Some teachers use the reading response journal as a

"No two persons ever read the same book."
— Edmund Wilson

How a Book Is Completed

In *The Spying Heart*, author Katherine Paterson (1990, 37) informs us that a "book is a cooperative venture. The writer can write the story down, but the book will never be completed until a reader of whatever age takes the book and brings it to his own story."

method of response. Some devise creative activities on their own based on curriculum needs, their students' needs, and the resources available in the classroom.

Traditionally, novels have been taught with the question-and-answer format. Students answer questions, prepared by the teacher or from commercial teacher guides, and the questions are taken up before students read the next chapter. Knowing what we do about personal response and authentic ways to respond to text, it seems that this traditional mode of instruction may provide neither an authentic way to respond to text nor a medium for igniting and supporting personal response. If questions were to be asked, breaking the novel into chunks, where questions are asked about different novel sections (e.g., Chapters 1 to 3), might be more acceptable.

Instead, we recommend considering the range of ideas found in an article titled "Literature-Based Reading Instruction: What's Guiding the Instruction?" by Lea M. McGee and Gail E. Tompkins. Each of us presents this article, which we are both fond of, in our Children's Literature course. Written about two decades ago (1995), the article outlines different approaches and activities that teachers employed to implement literature-based reading instruction. To explore the theory-based stage of literature implementation, the authors present plans for using the novel *Stone Fox* by John Reynolds Gardiner with students ages 9 through 12. The four plans provided are composites developed by groups of in-service and preservice teachers. They show connections among instruction, beliefs, and theory:

> Teacher #1 integrates social studies with the literacy goals/expectations and invites students to explore cash crops related to the topic.
> Teacher #2 includes *Stone Fox* in a unit she teaches on hero tales.
> Teacher #3 uses a reading workshop approach, where students collaborate in interest groups to read and respond to the novel.
> Teacher #4 uses a core literature approach, related to social studies, whereby students deepen their understanding of the Plains Indians.

In the article, theoretical perspectives on each teacher's plans are outlined, accompanied by teacher reflections. McGee and Tompkins do not argue that one perspective is "better" than another. Instead, they explore the benefits of a variety of theoretical perspectives on literature experiences. In their observations of classrooms, the authors found that teachers do more with novels than invite students' personal responses. They identified these four categories of teaching approaches:

1. *Encouraging students' personal responses to literature*
   Through questions and prompts, teachers invite students to discuss, write, dramatize, represent digitally, or use visual arts to convey their personal connections and emotional responses, remembered experiences, and other reflections of ways in which novels are or are not meaningful to them.
2. *Teaching reading comprehension skills*
   In guided reading or whole-class lessons, teachers do think-alouds or provide questions and prompts to show students the kinds of thinking involved in predicting, analyzing, synthesizing, inferring, and evaluating, as well as other comprehension processes that deepen their understanding of the novels they read.
3. *Raising awareness of literary elements*
   In guided reading or whole-class lessons, teachers highlight the author's development of plot, character, and setting, or other features of the novel, such as

the author's use of language or ways in which the author creates suspense through foreshadowing. In addition to enhancing students' understanding of a novel, teachers use the novel as a model for students' writing.

See "Critical Literacy in the Midst of Response" on pages 92 and 93.

4. *Engaging in critical reading*

   In whole-class or guided reading lessons, teachers point out and ask students to consider the social, political, and cultural assumptions, as well as the power relationships, revealed in novels. Teachers ask, for example, how students might feel about the characters if the story were told from an underdog's perspective. They also ask students to think about how authentically characters in the novels are depicted. Are there, for example, stereotypical patterns in the ways that characters from certain groups seem to be portrayed?

By drawing from each of the perspectives of McGee and Tompkins's framework when planning response activities to novels, teachers can feel confident that they are providing a comprehensive, well-rounded experience of the novels for students. All four of the perspectives provide opportunities for supporting students' literacy learning and enriching their experience with novels; the optimal approach, however, is to incorporate elements from each perspective whenever students respond to novels.

Exploring Comprehension Strategies

Effective readers use a range of strategies to build meaning and comprehend text automatically as they read. Sometimes, when we encounter difficulties understanding part of a novel, we can use different strategies to build our understanding of the text. Thinking about strategies is particularly helpful to make meaning and build confidence for purposeful reading. When teachers explain and demonstrate the use of strategies, then young readers can learn to apply these in a variety of combinations when interacting with text.

How Questions Can Promote Use of Strategies

Consider how this excerpt from Erin Bow's novel, *Plain Kate*, might be explored. The questions below the passage pertain to the very beginning of Chapter 1: The *Skara Rok*. As part of this activity, they are intended to provide teachers with models for uncovering a range of comprehension strategies. The excerpt can also be used with students in a mini-lesson to spark responses.

Source: From PLAIN KATE by Erin Bow. Copyright © 2010 by Erin Bow. Reprinted by permission of Scholastic Inc.

A long time ago, in a market town by a looping river, there lived an orphan girl called Plain Kate.

She was called this because her father had introduced her to the new butcher, saying, "This is my beloved Katerina Svetlana, after her mother died birthing her and God rest her soul, but I call her just plain Kate." And the butcher, swinging a cleaver, answered: "That's right enough, Plain Kate she is, plain as a stick." A man who treasured humor, especially his own, the butcher repeated this to everyone. After that, she was called Plain Kate. But her father called her Kate, My Star . . .

Questions that draw on key reading comprehension strategies:

- What stories do you know about superstitions and curses? (*activating prior knowledge*)

- What do you think this novel will be about? (*predicting*)
- If this were the opening scene in a movie, what images might you expect to see? (*visualizing*)
- What questions do you have about the story? (*questioning*)
- What connections might an orphan girl have to the *Skara Rok*? (*drawing inferences*)
- What words or phrases tell you that the father loves his daughter? (*analyzing information*)
- How has the text you've read [heard] help you understand that this story is set in a different time and place than modern life? Explain how. (*synthesizing*)
- The title of this chapter is "The *Skara Rok*." How might you read this title out loud? (*monitoring comprehension*)
- Rewrite the introduction in one sentence. (*summarizing*)
- How successful has Erin Bow been in catching your interest in the opening of her novel? (*evaluating*)

A Summary of Strategies to Support Comprehension

Students benefit from knowing strategies that meaning-making readers apply to their reading. Here is an overview of key comprehension strategies.

Activating prior knowledge: Ask: "What do you know about this topic? What does this remind you of?"

Predicting: Use experience, knowledge, worldview, and text features (titles, cover, summary) to consider what will come next.

Visualizing: Use words, structures, and meanings to create pictures in the mind.

Questioning: Ask questions to move the reading process forward. Doing so helps to become aware of the details that follow.

Drawing inferences: Use stated information and background knowledge to understand implied messages and to gain a deeper understanding of the text. In other words, read between the lines.

Analyzing specific information: Identify specific details.

Monitoring comprehension: Interrupt reading when meaning is lost and apply fix-it strategies, such as rereading or revisiting the text.

Synthesizing: Use and connect information from various parts of the text.

Evaluating: Make judgments by drawing on background knowledge, values, preferences, and text information.

A Structure for Response: Literature Circles

A Literature Circle is typically comprised of a small group of students who are reading a book and who meet to discuss, react, and share responses to it. When first establishing literature groups, the teacher may choose the same book for everyone to read. This pattern is most common. As time progresses, though, the teacher is wise to encourage students to choose among four or five titles that the teacher offers. These titles may be by the same author or on the same theme. When it comes to assigning books for Literature Circles, some element of choice should be given so that students have a measure of control over their own learning; however, this isn't always possible, since some books may be more popular than others.

The general purposes of the Literature Circle are to promote reading and response to literature through discussion and to allow students to work in small groups. To help facilitate their discussions, students are sometimes assigned roles. Often, the roles are introduced at the beginning phases and withdrawn gradually as students gain the social and communication skills to manage group work without assigned roles. The students can then experience a Literature Circle in a truly authentic way.

The Use of Roles within Literature Circles

To promote full participation in literature groups, some teachers begin by assigning roles which need to be explained and modelled; they then have students switch role duties after each session until the formal roles are no longer required. Students also benefit from demonstrations and exemplars of successful Literature Circles, where one group can serve as a model of how a Literature Circle can work or be improved upon.

Here is an outline of key roles:

Author Harvey Daniels offers support and a framework for implementing Literature Circles in the classroom. In *Literature Circles: Voice and Choice in the Student-Centered Classroom*, Daniels outlines the roles that help facilitate book talk. The context of Literature Circles provides students with the "kinds of things" to discuss when responding to books. However, Daniels argues that assigned roles should be used sparingly if students are to talk authentically about books.

- **The reteller** summarizes the reading for the group.
- **The instigator** raises issues for the group to discuss.
- **The linguist** draws the group's attention to interesting words or sentences in the novel (including the page number).
- **The literary artist** chooses an event or setting or mood conveyed in the reading and illustrates it for the group.
- **The questioner** presents puzzling issues, questions, or wonderings relating to personal response, as well as content for the group to consider.
- **The text enricher** supports the text by bringing in related stories or non-fiction articles or information from the Internet that can support or extend the novel's time, place, issues, and characters.

A wide variety of role sheets can be found on the Internet.

Beyond determining their responsibilities, it is important that students come prepared to each Literature Circle meeting. In support of assigned roles, they may need to prepare written notes or art. At the least, they will need to have read the agreed-upon material. Having each student keep a folder for role sheets and written responses is helpful to their being up-to-date with their reading.

Prompts for Guiding Discussion

To guide students as they participate in Literature Circles, the teacher may want to provide questions, such as the following.

- What do you predict will happen in the novel from the book cover? the summary? the title?
- Which characters do you find interesting? How so?
- Is the protagonist someone you care about? understand? connect to? Why is that?
- What questions do you hope will be answered later in the book?

• What do you find puzzling or out of place?

The teacher can also provide statement prompts, such as appear below, orally, on a chart, or on a Smart Board, to guide students on what they might contribute to book talks.

• Talk about the book's title, author, and style.
• Retell what has happened to this point.
• Talk about favorite parts of the book and reasons for these choices.
• Share connections to your own experiences or other books you've read.

Five Benefits of Literature Circles

Literature Circles offer five key benefits. They provide opportunity for students to take charge of their learning. They allow students to enrich their listening and speaking skills. They provide opportunities for students to deepen their comprehension by talking through ideas with others. Beyond that, students can learn from others' points of view. And all students have an equal opportunity to participate, which enhances their self-esteem and identities as readers.

Five Practical Considerations

1. To begin, you may want to assign students to a group. Once students become familiar with Literature Circles, however, groups can be formed according to novel choices. In this way, there may be readers of mixed abilities joined by a common text.
2. Ideally, three to five students want to read the same book, but when more students than that choose the same novel, several groups may be formed.
3. The teacher's role is to observe and evaluate, to solve problems, and to facilitate. The teacher monitors the groups and can participate in group discussions.
4. Literature groups usually meet three times per week for a period of 15 to 30 minutes; the sessions can last from one day to four or five weeks, depending on novel length.
5. Note that all the students in the class do not have to be engaged in Literature Circles at the same time.

Five Ways to Build Success

1. Have students use reading response journals as both a follow-up to a discussion and as a starting point for the next discussion.
2. Making a video recording of a session can help the teacher observe group dynamics and individual students' understanding of the novels. What's more, the group can view the video after completing discussions on the book and reflect on the process.
3. As a way to enhance their social and communication skills, students can reflect on the process and consider their participation and contributions. Discussion about the roles, the success of the roles, the preparation and contributions of each group member, and the use of journals can contribute to the success of Literature Circle meetings.

4. From time to time, have whole-class discussions to generate guidelines to help each student function and grow from the process.
5. Provide exemplars of best practices or an anchor chart with Literature Circle procedures and expectations. Students can refer to this information to determine how well they are meeting criteria for Literature Circle procedures (see "Success Criteria for Literature Circles," below).

Success Criteria for Literature Circles

I can . . .
- come prepared to a Literature Circle discussion by making notes according to my assigned role
- contribute ideas to Literature Circle discussions by making references to the book
- make connections to the book and to the responses of others, sharing personal stories and discussing other texts that I am reminded of
- willingly offer my opinion about the book and in response to contributions of others
- give evidence from the book to support my opinions
- be attentive when others contribute to the discussion
- successfully use my assigned role to present ideas about the book
- help facilitate discussion by asking questions, negotiating ideas, solving problems, and telling stories

---

FEATURE

"What Is the Holocaust?" A Literature Circles Approach

by Rachael Stein

This activity was adapted from the Yad Vashem Teaching resource: http://www.yadvashem.org/yv/en/education/conference/2004/61.pdf.

One February day, discussion in my Grade 7 class took a sharp detour. My students were making text-to-world connections using the movie *42*, an autobiographical story about baseball legend Jackie Robinson. One student compared the unfair, racist treatment of Jackie Robinson by many of the "white folk" to the treatment of the Jewish people by many of the Germans during the Holocaust. Another student bravely raised his hand and innocently asked, "What is the Holocaust?" A murmur of whispers around the classroom showed me that this was not the only student who had little or no knowledge about this critical and horrific time in history. So we created a KWL (Know-Wonder-Learn) chart to share our collective understanding of what we *thought* we knew about the Holocaust. My class was a diverse mixture of 32 students from different cultures and backgrounds, but even many of the 14 Jewish students had a limited understanding of the Holocaust. And so the theme for my next set of Literature Circles was born: The Holocaust.

Before jumping into the texts, I wanted to provide some contextual background for the students so that they could put themselves into the shoes of the characters in the text they selected. Students were told that they were going on a journey and might never return to their home. Each student was given an imaginary empty suitcase and only two minutes to "pack" anything from their home that they wanted to take. They were then directed to pick up their suitcase and find a place in the classroom all alone, away from their friends or anything familiar to them. They were asked: "How did this make you feel? What did you choose to take and why? How did it feel to be under such time pressure?"

I selected novels of a range of different text styles, protagonists, formats, and reading levels so that all of my students could access the Holocaust topic in a way that was meaningful to them. *The Book Thief* by Markus Zusak was the most popular selection for my stronger readers, while others (especially those who make selections based on text size) chose the fictional *Daniel's Story* by Carol Matas or the historical fiction book, *The Secret of Gabi's Dresser* by Kathy Kacer. For those who prefer different text formats, I included *The Diary of Anne Frank* and the graphic novel *Maus I* by Art Spiegelman. Each text employs a strong voice, whether of the protagonist or narrator, to retell the events happening to and around the character.

Literature Circle groups that consisted of five or six students met officially once a week for group discussion. During the week additional periods were designated for reading and keeping their individual fact logs up-to-date as well as for doing response activities. Instead of the traditional Literature Circle roles, group members had one common task: to record three facts that they learned about the Holocaust in the section just read. Each group meeting then began with members sharing what they learned followed by the group collaboratively completing a KWL chart. They then shared with the class a newly acquired fact and added it to our class chart. The class thus created a collective understanding of the Holocaust through the different texts.

In order to expand the class's understanding of the Holocaust beyond the texts, we extended our theme into the arts. Each week I would present to them a poem, a video clip, or an image to which they needed to respond and connect to their text. The Holocaust Memorial Day Trust website (http://hmd.org.uk/resources/poetry) provided a myriad of examples of poems. Yad Vashem's teaching guide also served as an excellent resource, presenting "Seven Poems, Seven Paintings" about the Holocaust.

Each poem or visual would be shared collectively on our Smart Board, and students, in their respective groups, would have a chance to discuss how it made them feel, how it related to their book, or how it connected to their lives, other world events, and other texts. Students would then pair-share their response with a member of another group.

The suitcase activity was brought back for the final group task. Each Literature Circle group was asked to choose items to pack in a suitcase for the protagonist from their text and to explain why each item was packed. As a cumulative individual assessment, each student was required to answer *"What is the Holocaust?"* — the question that had initiated our learning about the Holocaust through novels.

See http://www.yadvashem.org/yv/en/education/lesson_plans/poems_paintings.asp.

Critical Literacy in the Midst of Response

Reflective readers learn to look beyond the surface message of a novel to recognize the social and political viewpoints that are being communicated. They learn to examine the portrayal of particular characters or groups of people, identifying stereotypes and biases that place some characters in a more favorable light, perhaps because they appear smarter, stronger, or kinder, for example. Stereotypes and biases may be based on race, ethnicity, gender, religion, socio-economic or occupational status, language, ableness, or sexual orientation. For example, farmers have been positioned as brutish fiends mercilessly ending the lives of domestic and wild animals since the days of Farmer McGregor in Beatrix Potter's *The Tale of Peter Rabbit* (1903), through to Fern's uncle in E. B. White's *Charlotte's Web* (1952), and to the farmer who sent Audrey the cow to market in Dan Bar-el's *Audrey (Cow)* (2014). The farmer's perspective as a provider of food for the family and broader society and the difficult decisions made by the farmer could be taken up by students as they question the stereotypes propagated in

See "Novels with Alternative Perspectives: Multicultural Books" in Chapter 2.

anthropomorphic novels. Students can come to understand that authors construct their novels with the goal of influencing readers in some way — introducing a particular perspective on an issue or person or event; highlighting a theme that matters to the author; or providing entertainment and making readers feel good about themselves and the world. In other words, readers develop and refine critical literacy skills.

Ways to Approach Social and Political Perspectives

To deepen students' understandings of the social and political relationships and perspectives in novels, teachers can provide prompts and questions for students to discuss in Literature Circles or write about in journals. The following ideas draw on the work of Lewison and Van Sluys (2002) in ways that are most appropriate for the target age group for this book. Their dimensions of critical literacy provide a helpful framework for students' critical reading of all novels highlighted in this book and others on teachers' bookshelves.

1. *Questioning assumptions.* Students might question assumptions about what seems normal about the relationships among characters in the novel who are different because of race, ethnicity, gender, religion, socio-economic class, language, ableness, and sexual orientation, or they might, for example, identify how the relationships in the novel place characters in positive, powerful positions regardless of their race. Students might then compare and contrast these portrayals with experiences with people in their own lives and with media portrayals to draw conclusions about where assumptions about what is normal show up in their lives and the real-life experiences that belie the normalness of these perspectives.

   For example, encouraging critical analysis of *Charlotte's Web* might start by asking: "How often do you hear about farmers in the news? What impression do you have of the type of work farmers do? Where does your view of farmers come from?" (Students may mention movies, books, news, and family members.) "How does your impression of farmers compare and contrast with the way that E. B. White portrays farmers in *Charlotte's Web*?"

2. *Considering voices heard and not heard.* Students might look through the chapters to see whose voices are heard and who seems to be described by others, but does not have a personal viewpoint voiced. In *Charlotte's Web*, for example, students could identify how the perspective of Erin's uncle is represented and what impression readers form of him because of this representation.

3. *Consideration of alternative perspectives.* Students might take action and promote social justice by challenging the stereotypes and assumptions within the novel and considering how the story might change if told from other characters' perspectives or by critiquing stereotypical portrayals of particular characters in a review of the novel.

   In the case of *Charlotte's Web*, students could invite a livestock farmer to talk about her or his work and lifestyle and the questions, concerns, and issues that are inherent in farming. They might then rewrite a section of *Charlotte's Web* from the farmer's perspective, perhaps creating a Readers Theatre script for a podcast that presents alternative views on the lives and decisions of farmers. Such a response activity will extend and enrich each reader's interaction with the text, including the reader's appreciation of critical literacy issues.

How Diverse Are Children's Novels and Our Preferences for Them?

by Ernest Agbuya

Ernest Agbuya is a Grade 6 teacher at Queen Victoria Public School in Toronto.

Because novels are such an immersive media form, we can never underestimate the power they can have on our sense of where we fit into the world around us. When we are young, novels reflect our own experiences and show us the experiences of others. But how much do novels reflect reality? And exactly whose stories are told? Whose stories are relegated to supporting roles, if they are told at all?

This past year teaching a Grade 6 class, I put a lot of emphasis on the expectation from the reading curriculum that students will "read a variety of texts from diverse cultures." Taking a look at the books they were reading, I began to wonder how wide the scope of experiences represented in the novels was. As a first-generation Filipino Canadian, I am all too aware that we barely exist in mass media and that our presence in novels is no different.

I had also let my class know that I expected them to read some "BHP" (Before Harry Potter) books this year. Some of them were indignant. "Do we have to? I can't relate to books if they're old," said one. "The language is weird like 'thou' if they're over fifty years old," said another.

Inspired by writers such as Chimamanda Ngozi Adichie (her TED Talk about the "danger of a single story" is wonderful) and Azar Nafisi (author of *Republic of Imagination*), I asked my class *who is represented in the books they read*. That launched us into a conversation about why it is important to have diverse reading habits. It was a no-brainer. My students knew without testing it out that whites are most likely to be the lead character in the novels they read. Estimates varied, but all agreed that more than half of the lead characters in their novels were white.

We then put our hypothesis to the test. Each student looked at two lists kept on our class wiki — the favorite books list and a log of books read during the course of the year — and categorized the main characters by race. We counted each book read as one discrete experience, so that each time a person listed Harry Potter, for example, that counted as a separate *reading experience*. Students worked in pairs to crunch the numbers and construct bar graphs. The results were surprising only insofar as most of us had no idea just how dominant white main characters were: they starred in 78 percent of their novels.

The next step was obvious. We all knew that we wanted to pull more information from our reading lists. Groups reconvened and as we brainstormed other bar graphs that could be made, the students broke away to collect information from one another. This part was a lot of fun, just listening to them as their data came into greater focus.

Sophia T. suggested a website on which the students could make easy bar graphs. As they finished collecting and tallying the results, they plugged their numbers into the website, created their bar graphs, and printed out the results:

- What is the race of secondary characters? (74 percent Caucasian.)
- What is the gender of the main character? (Students tended to read about main characters that matched their own gender, but girls were more flexible.)
- What are the genres of the books you read? (Twice as many fantasy as compared to realistic fiction.)
- What is the nationality of the authors? (69 percent American.)
- What is the race of the authors? (85 percent Caucasian.)
- What is the socio-economic class of the main character? (48 percent middle class.)
- When were your books published? (44 percent written in the last five years; 35 percent written in the first decade of the 2000s.)
- Where are your books set? (56 percent set in the United States and Europe.)

- What types of families are represented in your books? (61 percent were from a straight family.)
- How old is the main character? (48 percent were 13 to 19 years old.)

Once the students were done, they presented their graphs, explaining what conclusions they could draw from them. We also took note of any questions that arose from these conclusions. The questions, inferences, and conclusions they drew were so rich that I had to cut short their discussions that encompassed sociology, media theory, and much more. They had a lot to say and a lot to disagree with each other about!

We made a hallway bulletin-board display with our graphs. Around these, we attached a few "speech bubbles" on which students wrote the most important conclusions they drew from the graphs as well as any questions that arose from their interactions.

Here are a few of a great many questions students raised for inquiry.

During one of our discussions, we wondered whether they mostly read about white, middle-class protagonists because this was the dominant group in Canada and the United States. Finn approached me afterwards, wondering what people his age in Asia, for example, would read. Would their books reflect their own dominant culture, or would they resemble our statistics? I got in touch with a former student teacher who is now an administrator in an international school in Japan. He passed some of our main questions to a Grade 5 class. We were very surprised by the results which indicated that, aside from some popular *manga* series, their tastes in novels were quite Western and not dissimilar to our results. This information was a real eye-opener for my students who began to understand notions of *colonialism*, *hegemony*, and *privilege*.

I popped into Another Bookstore, a popular shop for many of my students, and told a friend who was working there about our project. I asked if she could recommend novels that would promote a broader sense of diversity. Intrigued, Arden showed me several titles. Talk led to a plan to bring the class in to share their findings and then search for books that promoted diverse points of view, something that this well-curated shop specializes in. Finally, they would write reviews of these books and the bookstore would post them on their website.

Having done a small unit on movie reviews and the conventions of that form, it was not a problem for students to write their book reviews. Part of the expectations was for them to briefly explain our project and their own findings and then show how their book adds to the diversity of viewpoints in the young adult novel market. The reviews were generally positive, the only problem being that many of them had a tough time keeping things brief.

It is hard to know how much this inquiry affected my class's reading habits. By Grade 6, their reading tastes were strongly ingrained. Change does, however, happen, and occasionally a student would proudly show me a copy of George Orwell's *1984* and say, "Look, I'm reading a BHP book!"

A Highly Personal Forum: The Reading Response Journal

A reading response journal (also called a "dialogue journal" or a "literature log") is a convenient and flexible tool whereby readers are helped to reflect on their reading and make comprehension visible. Keeping a journal invites readers to communicate and explore the ideas and feelings that a text evokes and to relate what they read to their own lives. Journals provide a more personal forum for responding to literature as students reflect; the response tools also provide a medium through which individual students make choices on how to respond to novels.

Reading response journals place readers at the center of their learning, serving as records of what the readers are thinking about texts. Journals provide space for learners to reflect on, interact with, and find personal meaning in works of literature. They encourage storytelling, questioning, imagining, and speculating. When used on an ongoing basis, they provide ongoing documentation about readers and their learning for both students as readers and for the teacher as audience and guide. A reading response journal is a powerful way to stimulate interaction among teacher, text, and learner.

Sharing journal entries with others can be entertaining and informative. A teacher, friend, or family member who reads selected entries can begin a dialogue with the novel reader by offering comments on the reader's responses, pointing out connections with their thinking and expressing their points of view. If the student sets up a journal entry as a letter, there is a particularly good context for someone to read and respond to it. It is not necessary that those who respond to journal entries have read the same text as the reader.

There are several ways in which the teacher can facilitate journal exchanges.

1. The teacher can set up a system where assigned reading buddies exchange entries.
2. The teacher can invite students to submit their journals for his or her reading. The activity can be structured so the teacher is responding to five or six journals at any given time.
3. Students can be asked to place Post-it notes on journal excerpts, thus inviting focused response to specific items.
4. Students can meet in groups of four or five to share entries of their choice, asking questions, making connections, or offering opinions of what has been offered.
5. The teacher may prompt students to share journal entries with a parent or other adult.

Any exchange of journals can lead to either written conversations or book talk, thus extending the reading response journal entry. When a trusted audience responds to the journal, the reader can clarify thinking about the story, raise questions to explore further, and make connections between the text and his or her life.

Novels as Examples of Craft

Well-written novels provide readers with the best possible models of narrative writing — they are real books written with real intent for real audiences. When reading a novel, students can learn a great deal about the craft of writing, and the author of the novel often serves as an excellent writing teacher. Students may observe how the author represents experience, borrow vocabulary for their own writing, and learn how to describe characters and setting. They may come to understand how to emphasize what is significant in terms of plot. They may also learn to present factual information and how to convey the main idea.

Suggested Journal Prompts

The following journal prompts can help students reflect on their independent leisure reading as they record responses to what they have read:

1. What did you enjoy (or not enjoy) about what you read?
2. What, if anything, puzzles you as you read the text? What do you wonder about?
3. As you read, what do you "see" in your mind?
4. What problems unfold in the novel? How do you think these problems will be resolved?
5. What words, phrases, sentences, or images made an impression on you? How so?
6. What interests (or does not interest) you about the characters in the novel?
7. How did the events and issues in the novel connect to your own experiences or those of someone you know?
8. What new information did you learn from reading this novel?
9. How do you feel about the way the author presented the story?
10. What did you wonder about as you read the novel? as you finished the novel?
11. What did you learn about yourself as a reader?
12. What might you tell others about what you read?

Students may choose to glue such a list into their reading response journals for reference.

Ten Ways for Students to Write about Their Reading

When we offer students opportunities to write about their reading or to experience activities drawn from their reading, we are explicitly integrating reading and writing in our program. When the writing is shared with an audience of peers or the teacher, we are building a talk-reading-writing connection which may lead to deeper thought about the novel. Although the reading response journal provides an ideal personal forum for response (and is noted again in the first idea below), there are many more ways in which students can respond in writing to what they read. Here is a summary of some of these ideas:

1. Jot reactions to a novel on sticky notes, in response journals, or on personal copies of the book.
2. Add entries to a cumulative class response list or T-chart, for example, to showcase new vocabulary or key questions raised.
3. Write a letter to a teacher, friend, or family member about a book.
4. List questions that come to mind for further discussion.
5. Transcribe book-talk conversations.
6. Describe in writing a novel's events, characters, settings, and conflicts.
7. Retell the story as a series of newspaper articles, fictitious letters, or diary entries.
8. Create a Readers Theatre script that focuses on one section or chapter of a novel. (See "Readers Theatre" on pages 115 and 116.)
9. Share opinions of the novel in a book review for others to read.

10. Write in role as a character that appears in the novel (e.g., create a character's diary entry, a letter to a relative, or a fictitious autobiography). (See "Journaling in Character," below.)

Journaling in Character

Imagine you are a character in the novel you are reading. Write a fictitious journal entry (entries) from the character's point of view. The in-role journal allows you to describe relationships and events in the character's life, the character's thoughts and feelings when dealing with problems, or questions the character might have.

The activity described at right provides a viable — indeed, the best — alternative to the traditional book report. Refer to *Ban the Book Report* by Graham Foster, which argues vigorously against this activity.

For more than 15 years of instructing teachers, Larry has offered this assignment in the literacy course, and the results from the more than one thousand teachers who have completed the assignment absolutely shine. When students write as a character in a novel they have read, they can come to understand the thoughts, feelings, and conflicts another person might experience. Typically, the whole class responds to the same novel, or individual students could respond to independent reads. As applied to elementary and high-school students, this assignment can be given following independent reading time, where students retell in role something that happened in the novel they read.

Writing a journal entry from a character's perspective enables each reader to have a conversation with the text, thus giving the reader as much responsibility as the author in the making of meaning. In-role journals give evidence that students are able to enter the world of story, imagine themselves as other people, and begin to understand the thoughts and problems of these people. The fictional character created by the author is made all the more real for the students as they take on the *as if* perspective of that character. The writing-in-role assignment allows students to integrate reading, writing, and talk; build empathetic understanding by stepping into the shoes of others; reveal comprehension through an authentic context; dig deeply into plot, character, theme, and issues inherent in the novel; consider vocabulary, language, and style used by the author; retell story events in role; support personal response; and express ideas in writing in an open-ended way.

Sharing Responses

A significant feature of this literacy event is to have the students share their responses with one another. In this way, the assignment promotes a talk response to the reading and writing experience.

Students can write their journal entries about a single event in the novel or as a series of entries over time. In some cases, they might write entries from the point of view of an animal or an inanimate object. They can write by hand or by computer. They have the option of including illustrations.

Extension: As a follow-up to the main assignment, students can work in pairs to share their in-role writing with each other. To begin, one person silently reads his or her partner's writing and then interviews the partner who speaks in role as the novel character. The activity is then reversed so that each person has a chance to be interviewed. You may want to assign interviewers a particular kind of interviewing role (e.g., media reporter, neighbor, babysitter, or fellow employee).

Here are two journal entry samples by Grade 7 students:

In response to *The Giver* by Lois Lowry:
Dear Diary
Amazing day!
In our black and white world i saw red.

RED.

I am so amazed at the true colours that life offers. Then I started to think . . .
Colour . . .
     What does it mean.
Then I started to get curious.
I asked my mom, "What does colour mean?" She had a puzzled look on her face — as if she was waiting for this day to come.
I looked at my mother again and asked, "But what does it mean?"
She stared back. She rubbed her head, pausing to think.
Then she said, "Sit down Jonas . . ."

In response to *Egghead* by Caroline Pignat:
I hate how these people lack the comprehension of my intellectual understanding. It makes me furious that Shane thinks I told the principal that he's the one who bullied me. And so in front of my own locker and in front of my classmates, he beat me up. What would make him torment me? I'm so angry. I'm done for today. At least you listen to me, journal. My life is sad.

Other Contexts for Writing in Role

Beyond having students write a journal or diary entry from the point of view of a character, you could, regardless of the novel's time or setting, invite them to use their imaginations and write any of the following in character:

- a letter of advice to someone in the story (This letter could be written in the role of another character from the novel.)
- a letter to an advice columnist, describing a problem and articulating the feelings of the character (Two students who did this could then exchange letters and write back as the columnist offering suggestions on ways to handle the situation.)
- an e-mail from one character to another
- a message for a Facebook wall for a character in the story
- a newspaper or magazine report about a fictitious or real incident derived from the novel

FEATURE

Writing in Role: A Demonstration of Transaction between Reader and Text

by Brian Crawford

In Memory
Brian Crawford was a dear friend, colleague, and book enthusiast. Brian and I team-taught a Grades 3/4/5 family grouping at Silverthorn Public School in Mississauga. I miss our book talks and his humor. *L.S.*

The Grade 4 students' first experience with writing in the role of a fictional character grew in response to a novel that was read aloud to the whole class. After reading aloud a chapter in the middle of the novel *Abel's Island* by William Steig, I asked the students to imagine that they were the character Abel who had been stranded on the island and who was struggling to survive from day to day. I invited the students to consider that Abel might write to his wife Amanda to explain what was happening to him and how he felt about the experience. The following three letters demonstrate how the students were beginning to empathize with the character's dilemma by writing in role as Abel:

Dear Amanda,
Hi Sweetheart. This is Abel. I'm on the island across the water. I miss you sooooo much. I love you. If we were on this island together, by my side, it would be a lot better. Ever since I came over here, I've gotten to know myself a lot better. Being alone does that to you. I know that deep down I'm able to do anything

I try hard at. I think my name finally suits me because I'm 'able' to do more things.

> Love, Abel
> (Joanna)

Dear Amanda,
I hope I get across this island or I hope you find me. If you don't, look up into the sky on a clear night and you'll see a bright star. I'll be looking at the same star. When you look at the star, remember me because I am always remembering you and I hurt so much without you by my side.

> Love, Abel
> (Carson)

Dear Amanda,
I'm stuck on this island near the east side. I could be home sitting down, eating some cheese and crackers, drinking some cocoa and even watching my favourite TV show. If I wasn't here I would be sitting on the couch with you by my side filling me with warm kisses. If you would have tied your scarf on tight I wouldn't be here. BUT as you always said "everything happens for a reason."

> Yours truly
> Abel, the one and only
> (Natalie)

These sample entries reveal that students were able to write in the first person, imagine themselves as another — namely, Abel — retell story events, and enter into the problems and conflicts invented by the author, William Steig. With these initial attempts to write in role, students recalled plot details (*I'm stuck on this island near the east side*), but they were apt to be more inventive (*I could be home sitting down, eating some cheese and crackers, drinking some cocoa and even watching my favourite TV show*), make inferences (*I think my name finally suits me because I'm "able" to do more things*), empathize (*I hurt so much without you by my side*), and be reflective (*I've gotten to know myself a bit better. Being alone does that to you*).

With each student in role as Abel on the island, students came to better understand the isolation and desperation of the character in the story. Each entry in the class demonstrated a varied response that was initiated after listening to the same story. Each entry was a document of personal meaning that was brought to and taken from the story, thus demonstrating that writing in role can serve as a medium for trans-action between the text and the reader.

"The only important thing in a book is the meaning it has for you."
— W. Somerset Maugham

Responding through Talk

Talking about books can happen in both informal and formal ways. Book talks can be as informal as two friends meeting to discuss a novel that one or both readers have read. They can also be as formal as a whole-class discussion in which everyone talks about a novel they have read or heard the teacher read aloud. Some discussions can be tape-recorded and shared with others.

In small groups, discussion is often spontaneous. As in a Literature Circle, group members offer their comments, concerns, and criticisms in response to what they have read. Before reading, group members can gather to predict, anticipate, and set the stage for the novel's narrative. During and after reading, they can engage in purposeful talk to construct both personal and collective meaning.

Talk can also be the starting point for a variety of response activities. These range from research, role-playing, storytelling, brainstorming, questioning, writing, and reading aloud. As students probe a novel's narrative, they may revise their understanding and go on to create stories of their own in light of what other meaning makers reveal. Sharing thoughts and feelings with classmates who have read the same novels can lead to more sophisticated literary generalizations and deeper understanding.

Ten Contexts for Talk about Books

1. One student interviews another student about a novel he or she has read.
2. Pairs or small groups share opinions or enthusiasms about parts of a novel or the novel as a whole.
3. Students consult with others to plan and prepare a response activity.
4. Students form small groups to discuss a novel that all group members have read. (They may need the teacher's help in devising a framework for their discussion.)
5. In a small group, in which the teacher is a member, students discuss a novel that everyone has read.
6. The teacher leads a large-group discussion about a novel that has been read aloud to the class.
7. A student and a teacher share reactions, ask and answer questions, and make connections during a reading conference.
8. Students tell stories that come to mind as they read the novel. These stories can focus on events that have happened in their own lives or in the lives of others, or they can reflect events in the media.
9. Students meet with others who have not read the same novel to retell events and share reactions.
10. Students meet in Literature Circles, each taking on a role to discuss what they have read. (See "A Structure for Response: Literature Circles," on pages 88 to 91.)

Books as Films: Grist for Talk

Do you prefer to read a book before seeing the film version of it or after seeing the film version? The question is worth considering, especially since a good number of popular novels for young people have been transformed into the film medium. It can be argued that many people like to see a movie after reading a book, but perhaps the enthusiasm to read after seeing the movie is less — in any event, this topic works well for group discussion. The following questions may stimulate discussion with the whole class or in small groups:

• Did the movie meet your expectations? Did the work of the film makers please you? surprise you? disappoint you?
• How were the actors similar to or different from the characters portrayed by the author?
• What are some of the challenges of transforming a book into a film?
• What scene(s) that you hoped might appear in the film were omitted?

- Were the settings of the novel similar to what you imagined them to be?
- How did the techniques of film making enhance or detract from the story?
- Would you recommend this film to people who have not read the book? Why?
- If you had the opportunity, what would you recommend the director do to improve the film?
- Did seeing the movie spoil the book for you? Explain.
- Do you think the novel you are reading could be turned into a film? a play? a musical?

This last question acknowledges that a number of novels have been turned into musicals. Titles include three Roald Dahl works — *Matilda, Charlie and the Chocolate Factory*, and *James and the Giant Peach*; *The Lord of the Rings* by J. R. R. Tolkien; and *Tuck Everlasting* by Natalie Babbitt.

Responding through Art

Many readers enjoy representing their responses visually. By drawing, painting, making models, or constructing collages, students — especially visual learners — can convey their thoughts and feelings about a novel they have read.

For various reasons, including anxiety or difficulties with language, some readers are unable to respond orally or in writing. For these students, visual arts can offer a nonthreatening opportunity to express what they understand and appreciate about a novel and its elements. Illustrations and other art projects can serve as artifacts for group discussion and can help others understand what a reader is "saying" about the novel through the details, style, and emotions represented in the pieces of art.

Five Ways to Respond through Visual Arts

Some novels quite naturally invite students to respond through visual arts. As examples, for R. J. Palacio's *Wonder*, students can be invited to design the award given to Auggie for his bravery and courage; and in *Mr. Stink* by David Walliams, the text directly says here is what Mr. Stink looks like, which serves as a good invitation to draw.

Teachers may find it appropriate to provide ideas such as the following to their students.

1. You can explore plot, character, and theme through "Book in a Box." Find 8 to 12 artifacts that represent the characters and events in a novel you are reading. These items, which can include photographs, should help you tell the story of the novel. Ideally, they will fit into a shoebox or bag, which can be decorated with images representative of the novel. Practice telling the story by strategically ordering each item and explaining its significance; then, in small groups, each person can retell story events by referring to the artifacts.
2. Imagine that you have been hired as an artist to create illustrations for a novel you have read. What words or phrases from the text inspire a visual response for you? Which scenes painted a vivid picture in your mind? Which medium will you use to communicate your ideas? How will the use of different media (e.g., paint, markers, pencils, colored pencils, and pastels) complement,

change, or add to the style of the book? How will your illustration add new meaning to the verbal text?

3. Create a portrait mask for a character from a novel you have read. If you wish, cut out pictures from magazines or newspapers to represent events or symbols that reveal something about the character. For example, if the character was interested in music, the eyes could be made using pictures of instruments. The pictures you choose do not have to be taken literally; they could be symbols of events, relationships, or feelings of the character. Words and phrases can also be included in the mask design.

4. Film producers commission storyboards to help them structure the scenes in a film before it is shot. Create a storyboard showing a series of six to eight sketches representing plot highlights of one chapter or section of a novel. Your sketches could represent the most powerful images that a film audience would see. You may create additional panels to represent a scene, if you wish.

5. Imagine that a novel you have read is going to be made into a play or a film. The director has hired you to create a two-dimensional drawing that would represent a set described in the novel. If you prefer, you may construct a three-dimensional model set for a scene in your novel.

Responding through Media and Technology

Teachers can build on students' interest in using digital technology and media for information and communication when planning response activities to novels. The following activities are meant to use media and digital technology as tools for deepening students' engagement with and interest in the stories.

What's on the Playlist? Students in partners share songs they like listening to on their musical devices and explain why they listen. Do they identify with the lyrics? Is there a particular style or genre they prefer? They then think about the main character in a novel they have read and create a playlist of music and songs that they think this character would listen to, considering genre, lyrics, and musical influences. With the partner or in small groups, students can share their musical choices and discuss why their choices are important to the character and to novel themes.

Movie Trailers. Have students work in groups to create a movie trailer of a book using iMovie or Movie Maker. This activity allows students to synthesize and summarize a novel as well as to highlight significant characters and events from it. It is also a good way to promote and motivate others to read a given novel.

Portraits. Tagxedo is a program that allows students to create visual representations or portraits of characters from a novel. The computer application turns words or phrases into visual word clouds. The words are plugged in to create the picture. Students can choose from a recognizable outline shape that matches a character in which to insert words. They can also make portrait collages by using a computer program called Picasa.

The example at the top of the next page shows an outline of a light bulb that is a connection to the novel *The City of Ember*, where the author Jeanne DuPrau presents a society without any electricity.

YouTube Publicity Clips. Several publishers have created YouTube videos that present novel characters, identify the theme, and establish the plot in order to motivate readers to get the book and read it. You could show a clip to the class to invite students to wonder about a book and to read it, or ask students to find YouTube clips for novels they have read or for novels that are newly published. These YouTube clips can be shared and also serve as models for students to create their own publicity clips of books enjoyed. Checking out YouTube videos on *Wonder* by R. J. Palacio and *Saving Mr. Terupt* by Robert W. Buyea is a good place to start.

News Reports. Students may become media reporters, each creating a news report about an event in the novel. The report can take the format of newspaper article or feature, or perhaps be a videotaped interview between a TV reporter and someone in role as a character.

Media Promotions. Challenge students to create a PowerPoint or Prezi presentation to advertise the book. The PowerPoint might include significant novel excerpts and images that show the setting, characters, objects that symbolize events and relationships, and so on. What music might accompany the PowerPoint presentation?

Online Conversations. Set up a blog or wiki which students can use to have a conversation about novels. They can share their reactions and wonderings to a novel and invite others to share their viewpoints, too.

Twitter Feed. Students can practice summarizing and evaluating while imagining themselves at a significant novel event. Their task is to share the moment as it unfolds with Twitter contacts. They can write 8 to 10 Tweets, each a maximum of 140 characters. The Tweets should describe the event, the feeling of the crowd, and the event's impact.

Using Wikis to Support a Reading Program

by Ernest Agbuya

For two years I used blogs in my classroom until someone convinced me that wikis were a lot more versatile. For the last four years I have been using Wikispaces as the main communications hub for my class and their families.

Because I teach in the gifted program at my school, the majority of my students take the bus to school. As a consequence, I see parents a lot less frequently than I was used to. The wiki allows me to maintain a homework page on which I provide homework expectations, share important news and dates, and provide links to websites and videos both connected to and unrelated to curriculum. We are also able to send e-mails to one another through the wiki.

I was able to do most of this with blogs, but with wikis, all users are able to add and edit content on our site, not just me. As long as a user has permission, she can hit the edit button on a given page and add or change content. Once she hits the save button, a record, or "history," is kept, showing that she made the changes. The history keeps a list of every version saved. You can see what was added (highlighted in green) and what was deleted (highlighted in red) with each save. You can also revert back to old versions of a page, if needed. These features open up all kinds of possibilities for collaborative learning and community sharing.

When my students wrote book reviews, they were in charge of editing a partner's work. Each student created a page on which to write the book review. Once the rough draft was finished, partners were then able to go into edit mode and make any necessary changes, also commenting or providing suggestions. Once editing was completed, the writer could look at the history to see what changes were made.

I also do reading response letters on the wiki. Students write letters to me on their own page. When I get an e-mail through the wiki that the letter is ready for a response, I make any necessary edits to their work and then write a response. Since these letters are visible to other students, some will learn from the work of their peers and the comments I share.

Students are expected to monitor the changes made to any of their work through the history feature of each page. Each student has a page on which he or she lists areas of need in writing. For some, homophones such as *their/there/they're* present a challenge, while others have difficulty with sentence or paragraph structure. The strongest writers might have difficulty with being concise. Whatever their needs are, they keep a list of what they need to work on as well as helpful websites that can be used as resources. During "open language period" when we have the laptop cart, students have the option of working on what it is they need to improve as writers. When students are metacognitive of their strengths and needs, they can work at their own pace and self-direct their learning more effectively.

With careful guidance, clear expectations, and the ability of students to learn from one another, wikis allow for a great deal of independence and differentiation.

The following is an excerpt drawn from a set of reading response letters between me and Sophia A. Sophia was responding to the novel *Gregor the Overlander*, part of the Underland Chronicles by Suzanne Collins. She had done some research and found out that Collins was inspired by New York to write an urban take on *Alice in Wonderland*.

Sophia:
I think that Suzanne did a great job on an urban *Alice in Wonderland* feel and that taking a story that lots of people know, and modernizing and urbanizing it is a really good subject matter for a fiction book. (I took a mental note for

a fiction entry in my writer's notebook.) I'm assuming that's where she got the big cockroaches, spiders, bats and rats idea.

Teacher:
I really like that you had a question about when the book was written and then actually looked it up. I also liked how you took the fact that she was inspired by *Alice in Wonderland*. Now the Underland/Wonderland comparison really jumps out! But aside from the literal connections between those two books, are there any thematic text-to-text connections you can make between those two books?

Sophia:
In *Alice in Wonderland*, it's really literal, and she has to shrink and grow to get to where she wants to go. In *Gregor the Overlander*, he has to adapt to the new world, the new creatures and the Prophecy of the Gray. He must adjust to the different situations, and sometimes instead of looking at things just like the Regalian's, he must take a different view.

Teacher:
You certainly make valid comparisons. You have made me think about reading *Alice in Wonderland* again. I think Lewis Carroll would be pleased to read your message and know that his book has connections with 21st century reading.

Into a Character's Shoes: Dramatic Responses

Drama provides opportunities to step into the shoes of a character and to gain a better understanding of the character's dilemmas. By responding to a novel through drama, readers can express a character's innermost thoughts and explore a story from a variety of viewpoints, both orally and in writing.

The conflicts that arise in a novel can provide meaningful opportunities for students to work with others — in role and out of role — to solve problems, make decisions, and enact significant events. Even if the context is remote from the readers' experience in time or place, students can respond through drama to examine a character's actions, relationships, and predicaments. By improvising a situation portrayed in a novel, students respond as if the events created by the author are real. They step inside the author's fictitious world.

The text of the novel can also provide sources for dramatic interpretation. Readers can use narration and dialogue to develop scripts, monologues, or Readers Theatre presentations.

Five Ways to Respond through Drama

Teachers may want to offer any of the following individual, partner, or small-group ideas to students who have read a novel.

1. **Improvise a conversation.** Imagine that you can talk on the phone with a character from a novel. What questions might you ask? What advice would you give? Work with a partner to develop a conversation between the character and a friend, relative, or another character from the novel.

2. **Create a dramatic presentation.** With a small group of peers who have read and enjoyed the same novel, choose a scene to dramatize. It is recommended that the scene you prepare show the relationships between characters as well as a problem in the story. Decide on how the text will be narrated and how group members will role-play the characters for the presentation.

3. **Write a journal entry in role.** Imagine that you are one of the characters in the novel and that you keep a journal for reflection. Write at least one fictitious journal entry that would reveal the character's thoughts and feelings to events or relationships depicted in the novel. Or, if you prefer, create a series of journal entries to describe what happens over time. Writing in role in a journal will help you to understand how that character might feel about the problems, people, and events in a novel.

4. **Transform dialogue into a script.** Choose a section of the novel that features dialogue (minimum one-half page) and that interests you. The scene can be drawn from any chapter, but should provide important information to an audience unfamiliar with the story. Working in a group with others who have read the same novel, transform this dialogue into a written script that can be understood and performed by another group. You will need to make decisions about which characters to feature. How many characters will you need? How will you handle narration?

5. **Create a revealing dream.** Imagine that a character in a novel is having dreams about a problem or a past event (either troubling or pleasing). Work in a group to create a dream that reveals something important about the character and the story's conflict. Consider using music, movement (including slow motion), dance, sound effects, still images, and props.

From Chapter to Whole: Novel in an Hour

For more detail on such conventions as Story Theatre, tableaux play, and soundscapes, you may want to check out *Dramathemes*, fourth edition, by Larry Swartz. This book also features detailed drama lessons using a novel:
- *Mr. Stink* by David Walliams (Chapter 6)
- *Wonder* by R. J. Palaccio (Chapter 8)

Novel in an Hour is a useful activity for having students dig collaboratively into a novel that they have not all read from start to finish. The class is divided into small groups so that each group is responsible for conveying key information from one chapter of a novel. Depending on group size, some chapters can be eliminated from the presentation.

After reading its assigned chapter, each group makes a decision about how to depict the chapter's plot and themes. They might choose storytelling in role, Story Theatre, Readers Theatre, tableaux play, soundscape, dance drama, and improvisation. They may want to bring in props, musical instruments, songs, and simple costumes, which can sometimes enhance the dramatic presentation.

After preparing and rehearsing, each group, in sequence, presents its chapter to the rest of the class to create a Novel in an Hour (or perhaps two hours). Sometimes, the teacher may then have groups revise, rehearse, and polish their work to create a performance of the novel. Ultimately, the goal is to motivate students to read the novel in its entirety.

The novels listed below are recommended for Novel in an Hour because they have short chapters, present strong relationships, and explore the themes of belonging and dealing with adversity:

- *Night John* by Gary Paulsen
- *Stone Fox* by John Reynolds Gardiner
- *Sarah, Plain and Tall* by Patricia MacLachlan

Revealing Understanding: Activities

The following provides some suggested response activities that integrate reading, writing, talk, and arts responses to literature. These activities are suitable for almost any novel.

Activity 4-1: A Handy Outline

Here is one way to engage students in making inferences about the plot of a novel read.

1. Direct each student to place a hand palm-down with fingers spread out on a blank piece of paper and to trace around the hand.
2. On each finger in the drawing, students list an exciting event from the novel.
3. In the space between each finger, students list an event that they think is important but less exciting than those listed on the fingers. They will now have a total of nine events.

Extension: Students work with one or two classmates who have read different novels and use their hand outlines to retell significant events from the books read.

Activity 4-2: That Reminds Me Of . . .

Invite students to make connections between the novel they are reading and the people, places, and events that are familiar to them. When they record these connections, they may refer to the categories given below, but need not (and likely cannot) respond to all of them. When students can connect a memory in their lives with an incident in the novel, they should briefly identify it and list the page reference.

    People in their life
    Relationships they have had
    Adventures or incidents from the past
    Adventures or incidents that happened to someone they know
    Places they have visited
    Conversations they have had
    Feelings they have had
    Problems or conflicts with which they are familiar
    Other people's experiences
    Other books read
    Films or television shows seen
    World events from the past
    Recent news events

Extension: Have students work in groups to share connections they have with a novel they have read. Group members may have read the same novel, or not. Tell the students that, as they share stories about connections made, other group members may tell stories that they are reminded of, too. Remind them to explain how the novel inspired these connections.

Activity 4-3: Deal the Cards

"Deal the Cards" involves students in writing novel plot summaries and in determining important ideas. For this activity, each student will need 12 file cards (or 12 sheets of paper). On each file card, the student writes one or two sentences that describe an important event in the novel. Once the writing is completed, the cards should be mixed up so that they are out of order.

Students then work with a partner who has read a different novel. Each person is challenged to arrange the 12 cards — that is, 12 events — listed by his or her partner in a correct sequential order.

Tell the partners to take turns retelling the story of the novel they read using the 12 file cards as cues. It is important to connect the events by explaining how or why one event led to the next.

Activity 4-4: 100 Words

"A Novel Pyramid," on page 113, provides an opportunity for students to distil what they think of a novel into 36 words. Students then use their notes to discuss the title they read with at least one other person who has read a different novel.

"100 Words" provides another opportunity for students to summarize, this time by creating a synopsis, or book blurb, that tells others about the novel read. One purpose of a book synopsis is to interest others in the book, to persuade them to read it, so there needs to be a balance between highlighting the plot and problems of the novel and not giving too much away. When preparing a novel synopsis, the writer needs to

- summarize the plot
- explain the major conflict
- describe the characters and their relationships to one another
- highlight the main theme(s) of the novel

1. Direct students to prepare a synopsis of the novel by writing a summary that is exactly 100 words. Doing so means that students will continue to revise and edit and endeavor choose the best words possible to inform others about the novel.
2. Once their book blurbs are completed, students find a partner who has written a synopsis for the same novel. Partners compare ideas and then combine them to make a new summary exactly 100 words long.

Extension: As a class, students can post these synopses on a class website to inform and invite others to read the recommended books.

Activity 4-5: Going Graphic

This plot-focused activity provides a way for students to make inferences and synthesize events while responding to a novel through use of technology and visual arts.

Ask students to imagine that the novel they are reading is going to be transformed into a graphic story or comic. Prompt them to choose a significant event from the novel and to create a graphic page featuring six to eight panels to tell the story. For the graphic presentation, they might consider these questions:

- Which characters will appear in the illustrations?
- Will the panels show a scene up close, at a middle distance, or far away?
- How will the setting of the story be captured?

- How will narrative captions be used to tell the reader what is happening in some panels?
- Who will be speaking in speech bubbles? Will there be thought bubbles?

Students may wish to use a computer program (e.g., Comic Life) to help them create their graphic stories. If more than one classmate has read the same novel, students can work collaboratively to create a graphic story drawn from a single chapter or several chapters. They can create a comic longer than six to eight panels, if desired.

Activity 4-6: Text-Message Conversations

This activity affords students an opportunity to focus on character and plot while drawing on technology and media literacy to make inferences.

Students select an important or pivotal event or moment in the novel and create an imaginary text-message conversation between two characters from the novel. The conversation might describe or comment on the significant event.

To help them prepare for this activity, have students consider their own text-message conversations so that they duplicate the style and form of a message conversation. Tell them that they should also consider the way the character would text, as well as vocabulary and expressions the character would use as evident in the novel.

Extension: Students can work in pairs to read their conversations aloud and share with the class, thereby giving the class a sense of the characters and issues. The conversations could also be recorded or posted.

Activity 4-7: Movie Producer's Pitch

This activity, focused on a novel as a whole, invites students to promote a novel that they have enjoyed through writing and use of media. Students can work in pairs, in groups of three to five, or as a whole class to make their pitches. By stepping into role as movie producers, they can review and celebrate a novel they have read while the individuals or groups they partner with go into role as directors. Ideally, each group making a pitch has read something that the others have not. Students will have opportunities to practice the comprehension strategies of synthesizing and making inferences.

As an alternative to small groups presenting pitches to each other, each group could present its ideas to the teacher in role as director. In this way, sharing pitches becomes a whole-class activity, and the students can hear all the other groups' pitches. As they present, they should be challenged to convince the director how a movie based on their chosen novel would appeal to an audience.

The line master on page 114 outlines what students need to consider when drafting their persuasive pitches.

Activity 4-8: Calling a Help-Line Adviser

This activity is modeled on call-in radio programs where listeners ask for advice from an expert doctor or social worker or on help lines, such as Kids Help Phone, established to guide troubled youth who seek assistance. It allows students to delve into novel character and theme through the strategies of summarizing, making inferences, and evaluating. Both guidance and drama are curriculum connections.

Students work in pairs. One partner takes on the role of a character from a novel they have read. The other partner takes on the role of the support line worker or adviser on the radio. The novel character has made the decision to make the phone call and get advice about how to proceed. Each student in that role provides as much background information as possible by describing events and relationships that appear in the novel. The student in role as adviser should be prepared to ask as many questions as needed to understand the problem before offering advice on how to deal with it.

Each partner should have a chance to role-play the adviser and a novel character.

Extension: Allow students to choose one of their dramatized scenes to present to an audience, either another pair or the whole class. These scenes can serve as case studies to demonstrate some tough issues drawn from life. After watching a scene, students can discuss strategies for dealing with the issues central to the novel. The questions below can be used to consider the issues presented:

- How did the character come to be in the circumstances?
- What advice might be given to deal with the problem?
- Who might the character speak to about the problem?
- What are some of the challenges of having this conversation?
- How might this person help deal with the problem?

An alternative way to present these scenes is to videotape a conversation between a troubled youth and a social worker. The videotapes can serve as case studies to present to others.

Activity 4-9: Designing a Character's Bedroom

One way to understand a character in a novel is to think about where he or she lives. This activity offers a way for students to focus on a novel's character through the visual arts. Students have opportunities to visualize and make inferences.

To prepare for this art activity, students list information that they know about a central character from the novel they have read. They may consider words to describe the character's personality, personal relationships, hobbies, interests, possessions, skills and talents, and accomplishments.

Students then use this information to create a two-dimensional drawing of the bedroom that this character might have. They may want to use the Internet to find and modify images to help create the bedroom. These questions may help them to develop their illustrations:

What posters or pictures might appear on the walls?
What books might be in the room?
What equipment, souvenirs, or gifts received might be on display?
What kind of bed would the character sleep on?
What other furniture would be in the room?
Is the room tidy or messy?
What colors would be favored?

Extension: Once students have completed their drawings, let them share the drawings in groups. For this activity, each student can be a tour guide to describe and explain what is in the character's bedroom, what it might look like, why it is in the bedroom, and why something is significant to the character.

Activity 4-10: Location! Location! Location!

Imagining that the novel they have read is going to be made into a television mini-series is a way for students to focus on novel setting.

In a mini-series, there will likely be many different settings where the action takes place, so choices will have to be made. Tell students to think of themselves as location managers hired to recommend different locations where the film will take place. Some of these settings will be real; others might require the building of sets. Ask: "If you were the location manager for a film of your book, what settings do you think would be required to make the movie?"

Tell students that the cost of including all locations would be expensive, so they will need to decide which scenes from the novel are essential and which can be excluded. Responding to the following questions and statements will help them identify and consider the importance of the novel's settings:

Where did most of the action take place?

What location would be easiest to produce?

List scenes that took place outdoors.

List scenes that took place indoors.

What scenes could be eliminated or combined with other scenes?

Extension: Invite students to provide an illustration of *at least one* setting that would be required for the filming of this novel. This illustration will help the director and the set designer for the production of the film.

Activity 4-11: Readers Theatre Presentation

Readers Theatre is a literature-based ensemble activity whereby participants have authentic reasons to interpret and practice delivering a text in order to give a polished presentation. Preparing a presentation based on a novel engages students in considering an author's writing style and choice of language. Readers Theatre connects with the drama curriculum. A detailed student line master sets out a Readers Theatre activity for students on pages 115 and 116.

Activity 4-12: Capturing Voice

Students focus on style and language when they consider the effects of writing a novel in either first-person voice or third-person voice. In this exercise, they use the comprehension strategy of making inferences as they rewrite a novel excerpt in alternative voice and discuss the effects of changing voice with a partner. The line master on page 117 discusses first-person and third-person voice and outlines the activity in detail.

A Novel Pyramid, or, The 36-Word Book Report

You will be given an opportunity to discuss the novel you have read with someone who has read a different novel than you did. To prepare for the conversation, complete the following outline to summarize and give your opinions of the novel you are going to talk about. You have just 36 words.

_____

_____ _____

_____ _____ _____

_____ _____ _____ _____

_____ _____ _____ _____ _____

_____ _____ _____ _____ _____ _____

_____ _____ _____ _____ _____ _____ _____

_____ _____ _____ _____ _____ _____ _____ _____

ONE word that explains the theme of the novel

TWO words that give your opinions of the novel

THREE words that describe the setting

FOUR words that describe your opinion of the main character

FIVE names of characters

SIX words you learned by reading the novel

SEVEN words that summarize the main problem of the novel

EIGHT words that summarize the plot — that is, what the story is about

Once you have filled in a pyramid, meet with one or two others who have also completed a novel pyramid but for different novels. As you discuss your book, provide reasons for your choice of words for the pyramid. Although this 36-word graphic summarizes the novel succinctly, you should be prepared to answer questions and say more about the characters, plot, and problems of the novel.

Pembroke Publishers © 2015 *"This Is a Great Book!"* by Larry Swartz and Shelley Stagg Peterson ISBN 978-1-55138-308-8

Movie Producer's Pitch

Imagine that a movie director is interested in making a new film (or television movie) about young people, and consider that the novels you have read can serve as significant stories for movie production. Imagine, too, that you are a movie producer in the position to recommend a book on which to base the film. Before you meet the director, you are to prepare a sales pitch for the title you believe would work well. Refer to the following outline as you think about outlining significant features of the film.

- *Synopsis:* Summarize the story in 50 words or less.

- *Cast of Characters:* List the important characters. What are some words to describe each character? (You may also wish to suggest actors or actresses to play these roles.)

- *Setting:* Where will most of the movie take place?

- *Target Audience:* Who might be interested in seeing this movie? Why?

- *Lesson(s):* How might this story help audiences understand problems and issues of teenagers? Is there a lesson(s) to be learned? How is the movie true to life (or not)?

- *Significant Scene:* Describe one scene that might be particularly appealing for a movie audience.

Once you have completed the written sales pitch, you can meet in small groups to present your ideas.

Note: You may want to design a poster for promoting your movie idea. The poster could feature a scene from the novel.

_____

_____

_____

_____

_____

_____

_____

_____

Pembroke Publishers © 2015 *"This Is a Great Book!"* by Larry Swartz and Shelley Stagg Peterson ISBN 978-1-55138-308-8

Readers Theatre

In Readers Theatre, a script is developed from material not initially written for performance. The technique of Readers Theatre allows participants to dramatize narration and dialogue using selections such as novel excerpts, short stories, or fables. Readers Theatre does not require participants to memorize a selection, but before reading the text aloud, group members should think about and discuss the way narration and dialogue can be divided among them.

Work with a group with three to five classmates who have read and enjoyed the same novel. You will each need a copy of the book.

1. To begin, discuss scenes that everyone in the novel enjoyed.

2. Discuss which scene you think might be best dramatized for an audience through Readers Theatre. The scene should be no more than two pages. You will have a chance to transform this scene into a Readers Theatre script.

Here is an example of how a Readers Theatre script could look like, using an excerpt from the novel *Walking Home* by Eric Walters (page 88):

Just then three soldiers came into view. I didn't know two of them but the sergeant was the third. I waved and he waved back.

"Good afternoon, my young friend," he said.

"Good afternoon, sir. I was wondering if you have the time, could I ask you some questions?"

"Certainly." He turned to the other two soldiers. "You will continue your rounds and I will meet you at your next circuit.

Readers Theatre version:

Narrator #1: Just then three soldiers came into view.

Narrator #2: I didn't know two of them, but the sergeant was the third. I waved and he waved back.

Sergeant: Good afternoon, my young friend.

Muchoki: Good afternoon, sir. I was wondering if you have the time, could I ask you some questions?

Sergeant: Certainly.

Narrator #1: He turned to the other two soldiers.

Sergeant: You will continue your rounds and I will meet you at your next circuit.

Readers Theatre (continued)

Writing a Readers Theatre Script

With your three to five classmates, you will transform the novel excerpt you have chosen into a Readers Theatre script, which you will then rehearse and present to an audience. It is intended that each word of the text will be read, but you can cut text that does not add meaning. To begin, consider which lines are dialogue and which are narration. Keep in mind, too, that each person in the group should have more than one part to read out loud.

As you prepare the script, think about the following:

- Who will read each part? (As you rehearse, you can take turns playing the different parts.)

- Do you think you need to revise the script you have written? Go ahead!

- Will every word be spoken? Will you include such phrases as "he asked," and "answered the turtle"?

The following points will guide you through the process of exploring Readers Theatre.

1. Determine lines of dialogue and lines of narration to help figure out which parts need to be read by different performers. It is best if each group member has about the same number of lines to read out loud. A reader can take more than one part.

2. Decide how many narrators you will have.

3. Consider whether *every* word will be spoken. Will you change any words? You may need to make changes to your script. Doing so is fine! You will want to ensure that the story you are telling engages an audience.

4. Once scripts have been prepared, ensure that every group member has a copy. Volunteers can choose different roles. During the rehearsal, group members may want to try out different parts.

5. Once parts have been finalized, take a colored pencil or highlighter marker to signify which reading part is yours.

As you prepare to present, consider these questions:

- How will you engage your audience to listen and watch you as performers?

- Are you and the other members of your group each familiar with your parts?

- How will you stand or sit to best present your Readers Theatre piece?

- Will you always rely on reading the text from the page?

- How might your group go beyond traditional Readers Theatre? Are tableaux, movement, or choral reading possibly appropriate?

Pembroke Publishers © 2015 *"This Is a Great Book!"* by Larry Swartz and Shelley Stagg Peterson ISBN 978-1-55138-308-8

Capturing Voice

Novels are mostly written in first-person or third-person voice. A novel written in first-person voice will relate events of the novel through the eyes of a main character. This voice tells the story using the pronoun *I*. Here is an excerpt from the opening to the novel *Wonder* by R. J. Palacio, written in first-person voice.

> I know I'm not an ordinary ten-year old kid. I mean, sure, I do ordinary things. I eat ice cream. I ride my bike. I play ball. I have an Xbox. Stuff like that makes me ordinary, I guess. And I feel ordinary. Inside.

A novel written in third-person voice will relate events through the eyes of someone outside the novel's action. This voice tells the story using the pronoun *she* or *he* (or maybe *they*). Here is an extract from the opening to *The Turtles of Oman*, a novel by Naomi Shihab Nye, which is written in third-person-voice.

> Aref Al-Amri stared at the Muscat International Airport security guards. They looked very serious in their brown uniforms, checking tickets waving travelers forward. He was standing with his parents. His dad hadn't stepped into the security line yet.

Novels are not written in second-person voice, which uses the pronoun *you*. Writing in this voice is found in instructions or directions, not usually in fiction writing.

Select an excerpt of about half a page from a novel you are reading. If the novel is written in first-person voice, rewrite the passage in third-person voice. If the novel is written in third-person voice, rewrite the passage in first-person voice. As you rewrite, you will need to change certain words to match the voice. Keep the tone of the passage as authentic as possible.

Once you have finished rewriting your passage, share it with a partner. Discuss:

- How are novels written in first-person voice similar to or different from those written in third-person voice?

- Generally, which voice do you prefer reading? Why?

- In what ways does the story change by switching voices?

- What might readers learn about the character (and other characters) when first-person voice is used?

- What might readers learn about the character when third-person voice is used?

Appendixes

Leisure Reading List by Top 10 Titles

The titles in this list are all from the 21st century and are organized by age and genre. The "also" and "sequel" listings reflect an effort to share as many key titles by favorite authors as possible!

CHAPTER BOOK SERIES (AGES 7 TO 9)

Ivy and Bean by Annie Barrows

Beast Quest by Adam Blade

Bad Kitty by Nick Bruel

The Adventures of the Bailey School Kids by Debbie Dadey and Marcia Thornton Jones

The Life of Ty by Lauren Myracle

Nancy Clancy by Jane O'Connor

My Big Fat Zombie Goldfish by Mo O'Hara

The Magic Tree House by Mary Pope Osborne

Geronimo Stilton by Geronimo Stilton

Judy Moody by Megan McDonald (Also: *Stink*)

NOVELS (AGES 10 TO 12)

Home of the Brave by Katherine Applegate (Also: *The One and Only Ivan*)

Because of Mr. Terupt by Rob Buyea (Sequels: *Mr. Terupt Falls Again, Saving Mr. Terupt*)

Flora & Ulysses by Kate DiCamillo (Also: *The Miraculous Journey of Edward Toulane*)

Out of My Mind by Sharon M. Draper

Stir It Up! by Ramin Ganeshram

Escape from Mr. Lemoncello's Library by Chris Grabenstein (Also: *The Island of Dr. Libris*)

Fuzzy Mud by Louis Sachar

The Crazy Man by Pamela Porter

Wonder by R. J. Palacio (Also: *Auggie & Me: Three Wonder Stories*)

A Long Walk to Water by Linda Sue Park

NOVELS (AGES 12 TO 15)

Thirteen Reasons Why by Jay Asher

The Perks of Being a Wallflower by Stephen Chbosky

The Eye of Minds by James Dashner (Also: *The Rule of Thoughts*)

The Fault in Our Stars by John Green

All the Bright Places by Jennifer Niven

Miss Peregrine's Home for Peculiar Children by Ransom Riggs (Sequel: *Hollow City*)

Counting by 7s by Holly Sloan

It's Kind of a Funny Story by Ned Vizzini

Code Name Verity by Elizabeth Wein

The Book Thief by Marcus Zusak

BOOK SERIES

Popular Adventure Series for Younger Readers (Ages 9 to 12)

The Origami Yoda Files by Tom Angleberger

Animorphs by K. A. Applegate

The Land of Stories by Chris Colfer

Artemis Fowl by Eoin Colfer

Creepover by P. J. Night

Seven (the Series) (various Orca Book authors)

Kingdom Keepers by Ridley Pearson

Stranded by Jeff Probst and Chris Tebbetts

Percy Jackson & the Olympians by Rick Riordan (Also: Heroes of Olympus)

The 39 Clues (multi-authors)

Popular Series for Older Readers (Ages 12 to 15)

Graceling Realm by Kristin Cashore

The Mortal Instruments by Cassandra Clare

The Hunger Games by Suzanne Collins

The Maze Runner by James Dashner

I Am Number Four by Pittacus Lore

Vampire Academy by Richelle Mead

Lunar Chronicles by Marissa Meyer

The Twilight Saga by Stephenie Meyer

Divergent by Veronica Roth

The Uglies by Scott Westerfeld

GRAPHIC NOVEL SERIES

Babymouse by Jennifer Holm and Matthew Holm

Amulet by Kazu Kibuishi

Pembroke Publishers © 2015 *"This Is a Great Book!"* by Larry Swartz and Shelley Stagg Peterson ISBN 978-1-55138-308-8

Leisure Reading List by Top 10 Titles (continued)

Naruto by Masashi Kishimoto
Loser List by H. N. Kowlit
Amelia Rules by Jim Gownley
Diary of a Wimpy Kid by Jeff Kinney
Big Nate by Lincoln Peirce
The Adventures of Captain Underpants by Dav
    Pilkey
Geronimo Stilton by Geronimo Stilton
Bone by Jeff Smith

RECOMMENDATIONS BASED ON CURRENT LIKINGS

If you like humorous contemporary series such as
The Diary of a Wimpy Kid by Jeff Kinney, try . . .

Dear Dumb Diary by Jim Benton
Cartboy by L. A. Campbell
The Popularity Papers by Lydia Goldblatt and
    Julie Graham-Chang
Middle School by James Patterson; illus. Chris
    Tebbetts (Also: I, Funny)
Timmy Failure by Stephan Pastis
The Winnie Years by Lauren Myracle
Tom Gates by Liz Pichon
Big Nate by Lincoln Pierce
Dork Diaries by Rachel Renée Russell
The My Life series by Janet Tashjian

If you like fantasy world stories such as the Harry
Potter series by J. K. Rowling, try . . .

The Night Gardener by Jonathan Auxier
Starcatcher series by Dave Barry and Ridley
    Pearson
Plain Kate by Erin Bow
Inkheart (quartet) by Cornelia Funke
Where the Mountain Meets the Moon by Grace
    Lin (Sequel: Starry River of the Sky)
Charlie Bone: The Children of Red King by Jenny
    Nimmo
The Inheritance Cycle by Christopher Paolini
The Hunchback Assignments (series) by Arthur
    Slade
This Dark Endeavor: The Apprenticeship of Victor
    Frankenstein by Kenneth Oppel
Septimus Heap (series) by Angie Sage and Mark
    Zug

If you like relationship stories such as The Fault in the
Stars by John Green, try . . .

Me and Earl and the Dying Girl by Jesse Andrews
If I Stay by Gayle Forman (Sequel: Where She
    Went)
Goodbye Stranger by Rebecca Stead (Also: When
    You Reach Me)
Looking for Alaska by John Green (Also: Paper
    Towns)
Every Day by David Levithan
I'll Give You the Sun by Jandy Nelson
All the Bright Places by Jennifer Niven
Eleanor and Park by Rainbow Rowell
The Impossible Theory of Ana & Zak by Brian
    Katcher
The Art of Being Normal by Lisa Williamson

A SELECTION OF NOTEWORTHY CANADIAN NOVELS

Ages 9 to 12

The Madman of Piney Woods by Christopher
    Paul Curtis (Also: Elijah of Buxton)
Lord and Lady Bunny — Almost Royalty by Polly
    Horvath
The Elevator Ghost by Glen Huser
Viminy Crowe's Comic Book by Marthe Jocelyn
    and Richard Scrimger
Better Than Weird by Anna Kerz
Ungifted by Gordon Korman
The Boy Sherlock Holmes by Shane Peacock
Egghead by Caroline Pignat
The Crazy Man by Pamela Porter
Walking Home by Eric Walters

Ages 12 to 15

Camp Outlook by Brenda Baker
Cut-off by James Bastedo
Plain Kate by Erin Bow
Diego's Crossing by Robert Hough
Nix Minus One by Jill MacLean
The End of the Line by Sharon E. McKay
We Are All Made of Molecules by Suzanne
    Nielsen
The Boundless by Kenneth Oppel (Also: Airborn)
Underground Soldier by Marsha Forchuk Skrypuch
Wings of War by John Wilson

Pembroke Publishers © 2015 "This Is a Great Book!" by Larry Swartz and Shelley Stagg Peterson ISBN 978-1-55138-308-8

From Chapter Books to YA Books: Recommended Titles

Chapter Book Series

Adler, David. Cam Jansen

Barrows, Annie. Ivy & Bean

Brown, Marc. Arthur

Dadey, Debbie, and Marcia Thornton Jones. The Adventures of the Bailey School Kids

Giff, Patricia Reilly. The Kids of the Polk Street School

Greenhut, Josh. Flat Stanley's World Wide Adventures

MacGregor, Roy. The Screech Owls

McDonald, Megan. Judy Moody

O'Connor, Jane. Nancy Clancy

O'Hara, Mo. My Big Fat Zombie Goldfish

Osborne, Mary Pope. The Magic Tree House

Park, Barbara. Junie B. Jones

Pennypacker, Sara. Clementine

Roy, Ron. A to Z Mysteries

Sachar, Louis. Marvin Redpost

Scieszka, Jon. The Time Warp Trio

Sharmat, Marjorie W. Nate the Great

Sobol, Donald. Encyclopedia Brown

Stilton, Geronimo. Geronimo Stilton books

Wishinsky, Frieda. Canadian Flyer Adventures

Fiction for Transitional Readers (Ages 8–10)

Avi. *The End of the Beginning* (Sequel: *A Beginning, a Muddle, and an End*)

Blume, Judy. *Tales of a Fourth Grade Nothing* (Sequels: *Superfudge, Fudge-a-Mania, Double Fudge*)

Byars, Betsy. *The Midnight Fox*

_____. *The Summer of the Swans*

Clements, Andrew. *The Jacket*

Dahl, Roald. *James and the Giant Peach*

_____. *Charlie and the Chocolate Factory*

_____. *Matilda*

_____. *The Twits*

Doyle, Roddy. *The Giggler Treatment*

Gardiner, John Reynolds. *Stone Fox*

Henkes, Kevin. *The Year of Billy Miller*

_____. *Sun & Spoon*

Howe, Deborah, and James Howe. *Bunnicula* (Sequels: *The Celery Stalks at Midnight, Howliday Inn, Nighty Nightmare*)

Little, Jean. *Different Dragons*

_____. *Lost and Found*

MacLachlan, Patricia. *Sarah, Plain and Tall* (trilogy)

Park, Barbara. *Mick Harte Was Here*

Richler, Mordecai. *Jacob Two Two Meets the Hooded Fang* (Sequels: *Jacob Two Two and the Dinosaur, Jacob Two Two's First Spy Case*)

Rockwell, Thomas. *How to Eat Fried Worms*

Rylant, Cynthia. *Missing May*

Scrimger, Richard. *The Nose from Jupiter* (Sequels: *A Nose for Adventure, Noses*)

Selden, George. *The Cricket in Times Square* (Sequels: *Tucker's Countryside, Harry Kitten and Tucker Mouse*)

Smith, Doris Buchanan. *A Taste of Blackberries*

Smith, Robert Kimmel. *Chocolate Fever*

Smucker, Barbara. *Jacob's Little Giant*

Viorst, Judith. *Lulu and the Brontosaurus* (trilogy)

Series for Transitional Readers
(Ages 8 to 10)

Cleary, Beverly. Ramona
Danziger, Paula. Amber Brown
Hale, Shannon. The Princess Academy
Hurwitz, Johanna. Aldo Applesauce
Korman, Gordon: Danger series (Trilogies: Dive, Everest, Island, Kidnapped)
Martin, Ann M. The Baby-Sitters Club
Pilkey, Dav. Captain Underpants
Sachar, Louis. Wayside School
Scieszka, Jon. The Time Warp Trio
Snicket, Lemony. A Series of Unfortunate Events

Fiction for Developing Readers
(Ages 9 to 12)

Applegate, Katherine. *The One and Only Ivan*
Armstrong, William H. *Sounder*
Avi. *Crispin* (trilogy)
Baker, Deirdre. *Becca at Sea*
Bar-el, Dan. *Audrey (Cow)*
Barton, Bob. *Trouble on the Voyage*
Birdsall, Jean. *The Penderwicks*
Boyne, John. *The Terrible Thing That Happened to Barnaby Brocket*
Buyea, Rob. *Because of Mr. Terupt* (Sequels: *Mr. Terupt Falls Again, Saving Mr. Terupt*)
Cameron, W. Bruce. *Ellie's Story* (Also: *A Dog's Purpose*)
Choldenko, Gennifer. *If a Tree Falls at Lunch Period*
Clements, Andrew. *No Talking*
_____. *The Janitor's Boy*
_____. *The Landry News*
_____. *Frindle*
Creech, Sharon. *The Castle Corona*
D'Adamo, Francesco. *Iqbal*
DiCamillo, Kate. *Flora & Ulysses*
_____. *The Tale of Despereaux*
Ellis, Deborah. *The Breadwinner* (trilogy)
_____. *Jakeman*
Erskine, Kathryn. *Mockingbird*
Gantos, Jack. *Joey Pigza Swallowed the Key* (Sequels: *Joey Pigza Loses Control, What Would Joey Do?, I Am Not Joey Pigza*, and *The Key That Swallowed Joey Pigza*)
Grabenstein, Chris. *Escape from Mr. Lemoncello's Library*
Graff, Lisa. *Lost in the Sun*
_____. *Absolutely Almost*
_____. *A Tangle of Knots*
_____. *The Thing about Georgie*

Griffiths, Andy. *The Day My Butt Went Psycho* (trilogy)
Henkes, Kevin. *Words of Stone*
Hof, Marjolijn. *Mother Number Zero*
Holm, Jennifer L. *The Fourteenth Goldfish*
Horvath, Polly. *One Year in Coal Harbour*
_____. *Everything on a Waffle*
Kadohata, Cynthia. *Kira-Kira*
Korman, Gordon. *No More Dead Dogs*
Lord, Cynthia. *Rules*
Martin, Ann M. *Rain Reign* (Also: *A Dog's Life*)
Morpurgo, Michael. *Born to Run*
_____. *War Horse*
Naylor, Phyllis Reynolds. *Shiloh* (trilogy)
Ness, Patrick. *A Monster Calls*
O'Connor, Barbara. *Greetings from Nowhere*
_____. *How to Steal a Dog*
Park, Linda Sue. *A Long Walk to Water*
_____. *A Single Shard*
Paterson, Katherine. *Bridge to Terabithia*
Patron, Susan. *The Higher Power of Lucky*
Rawls, Wilson. *Where the Red Fern Grows*
Ryan, Pam Muñoz. *Esperanza Rising*
Spinelli, Jerry. *Eggs*
_____. *Stargirl* (Sequel: *Love, Stargirl*)
Sloan, Holly. *Counting by 7's*
Steig, William. *Abel's Island*
Stewart, Trenton Lee. *The Mysterious Benedict Society* (Sequel: *The Mysterious Benedict Society and the Perilous Journey*)
Walliams, David. *Awful Auntie*
_____. *Demon Dentist*
_____. *Gangsta Granny*
_____. *Billionaire Boy*
_____. *Mr. Stink*
_____. *The Boy in the Dress*
Zimmer, Tracie Vaughn. *42 Miles*

Series for Developing Readers

Applegate, K. A. Animorphs
Clements, Andrew. Keepers of the School
Colfer, Eoin. Artemis Fowl
Hunter, Evan. Warriors
Kinney, Jeff. Diary of a Wimpy Kid
Russell, Rachel Renée. Dork Diaries
Lincoln Peirce. Big Nate
Nimmo, Jenny. Charlie Bone: Children of the Red King
Riordan, Rick. Percy Jackson & the Olympians
_____. The Heroes of Olympus
_____. The Kane Chronicles

_____.The 39 Clues (A collaboration of authors)

Young Adult Novels (Ages 12 to 15)

Avi. *Nothing but the Truth*
Beam, Cris. *I Am J*
Block, Frances Lia. *Weetzie Bat*
Blume, Judy. *Forever*
_____. *Are You There God? It's Me, Margaret*
Brooks, Marthe. *Queen of Hearts*
Cormier, Robert. *The Chocolate War*
Curtis, Christopher Paul. *The Madman of Piney Woods*
_____. *Elijah of Buxton*
_____. *Bucking the Sarge*
_____. *Bud, Not Buddy*
_____. *The Watsons Go to Birmingham — 1963*
Danziger, Paula. *The Cat Ate My Gymsuit*
Doyle, Brian. *Mary Ann Alice*
_____. *Easy Avenue*
_____. *Angel Square*
_____. *Up to Low*
Gantos, Jack. *Dead End in Norvelt* (Sequel: *From Norvelt to Nowhere*)
Gino, Alex. *George*
Green, John. *The Fault in Our Stars*
_____. *Paper Towns*
_____. *Looking for Alaska*
Hinton, S. E. *Tex*
_____. *Rumble Fish*
_____. *That Was Then, This Is Now*
_____. *The Outsiders*
Holman, Felice. *Slake's Limbo*
Johnston, Julie. *Adam and Eve and Pinch-Me*
Levithan, David. *Two Boys Kiss*
_____. *Every Day*
_____. *Boy Meets Boy*
_____, and John Green. *Will Grayson, Will Grayson*
Major, Kevin. *Far from Shore*
_____. *Hold Fast*
Makaelsen, Ben. *Touching Spirit Bear*
Myers, Walter Dean. *Shooter*
_____. *Monster*
Myers, Walter Dean, and Christopher Myers. *Autobiography of My Dead Brother*
Myracle, Lauren. *ttyl* (Also: *ttfn; l8r, g8r*)
Niven, Jennifer. *All the Bright Places*
Perkins, Lynn Rae. *Criss Cross*

Peters, Julie Ann. *Luna*
Polonsky, Ami. *Gracefully Grayson*
Riggs, Ransom. *Miss Peregrine's Home for Peculiar Children* (Sequel: *Hollow Café*)
Rowell, Rainbow. *Eleanor and Park*
Stead, Rebecca. *When You Reach Me* (Also: *Goodbye Stranger*)
Vanderpool, Clare. *Moon over Manifest*
Voight, Cynthia. *Homecoming* (Tillerman Cycle trilogy)
Walters, Eric. *Say You Will*
_____. *Shattered*
_____. *Stars*
Walters, Eric, and Deborah Ellis. *Bifocal*
Williamson, Lisa. *The Art of Being Normal*
Wynne-Jones, Tim. *A Thief in the House of Memory*
_____. *The Boy in the Burning House*
_____. *Stephen Fair*
_____. *The Maestro*
Zindel, Paul. *The Pigman*

Series for Young Adults

Andrews, V. C. Flowers in the Attic
Brashares, Ann. The Sisterhood of the Traveling Pants
Cass, Kiera. The Selection
Collins, Suzanne. The Hunger Games
Dashner, James. The Maze Runner
_____. The Mortality Doctrine
Harrison, Lis. The Clique
Lore, Pittacus. I Am Number Four
Lu, Marie. Legend
MacHale, D. J. Pendragon
Mead, Richelle. Vampire Academy
Meyer, Stephanie. The Twilight Saga
Nix, Garth. Sabriel (trilogy)
_____. The Seventh Tower
Paolini, Christopher. The Inheritance (trilogy)
Pierce, Tamora. Protector of the Small (quartet)
Pullman, Philip. His Dark Materials
Roth, Veronica. Divergent
Rowling, J. K. Harry Potter
Sage, Angie. Septimus Heap
Shan, Darren. Cirque du Freak
Stewart, Paul, and Chris Rideel. The Edge Chronicles
Stroud, Jonathan. The Bartimaeus Trilogy
Tolkien, J. R. R. The Lord of the Rings

Novels on Selected Themes

These lists encompass certain themes, including war, bullying, and multicultural perspectives.

Novels on the Theme of War

Lynch Chris. World War II: *The Right Fight* (trilogy)
Morpurgo, Michael. *Private Peaceful*
_____. *War Horse*
Pearson, Kit. *The Sky Is Falling* (Guests of War trilogy)
Walters, Eric. *War of the Eagles*
_____. Camp X (series)
Wein, Elizabeth. *Code Name Verity*
Wilson, John. *Wings of War*

Multicultural Novels

Alire Sáenz, Benjamin. *Aristotle and Dante Discover the Secrets of the Universe*
Baskin, Nora Raleigh. *Anything but Typical*
Bond, Victoria, and T. R. Simon. *Zora and Me*
Boyne, John. *The Boy in the Striped Pajamas*
Edwardson, Debbie Dahl. *My Name Is Not Easy*
Engle, Margarita. *Silver People: Voices from the Panama Canal*
Guest, Jacqueline. *Outcasts of River Falls*
Jordan-Fenton, Christy. *Fatty Legs: A True Story*
Kacer, Kathy. *Hiding Edith*
Little, Jean. *Willow and Twig*
Maccoll, Michaela. *Promise the Night*
Manzano, Sonia. *The Revolution of Evelyn Serrano*
Marsden, Carolyn. *My Own Revolution*
Molnar, Haya Leah. *Under a Red Sky*
Perkins, Mitali. *Bamboo People*
Pinkney, Andrea Davis. *Bird in a Box*
Preus, Margi. *Shadow on the Mountain*

_____. *Heart of a Samurai*
Rhuday-Perkovich, Olugbemisola. *8th Grade Super Zero*
Robertson, David Alexander. *The Ballad of Nancy April (Shawnadithit)*
_____. *The Land of Os: John Ramsay*
_____. *The Peacemaker: Thanadelthur*
_____. *The Poet: Pauline Johnson*
_____. *The Rebel: Gabriel Dumont*
_____. *The Scout: Tommy Prince*
Sepetys, Ruth. *Between Shades of Gray*
Skrypuch, Marsha Forchuk. *Underground Soldier*
_____. *Daughter of War*
Slipperjack, Ruby. *Little Voice*
Spiegelman, Art. *Maus* (Also: *Maus II*)
Spinelli, Jerry. *Milkweed*
Stewart, Elizabeth. *The Lynching of Louie Sam*
Williams, Michael. *Now Is the Time for Running*
Zusak, Markus. *The Book Thief*

Novels about Bullying

Anderson, Laurie Halse. *Speak*
Bloor, Edward. *Tangerine*
Blume, Judy. *Blubber*
Carone, Elise. *Starting School with an Enemy*
Chambers, Aidan. *The Present Takers*
Clements, Andrew. *Jake Drake: Bully Buster*
Fine, Anne. *The Angel of Nitshill Road*
Flake, Sharon G. *The Skin I'm In*
Gardner, Graham. *Inventing Elliot*
Giles, Gail. *Shattering Glass*
Hogg, Gary. *Scrambled Eggs and Spider Legs*

Howe, James. *The Misfits*

Jackson III, Curtis "50 Cent." *Playground: The Mostly True Story of a Former Bully*

Jordan-Fenton, Christy, and Margaret Pokiak-Fenton. *Fatty Legs*

Kerz, Anna. *Better Than Weird*

Koss, Amy Goldman. *Poison Ivy*

Maciel, Amanda. *Tease*

Mackall Dandi Daley. *Larger-Than-Life Lara*

MacLean, Jill. *The Nine Lives of Travis Keating*

_____.*The Present Tense of Prinny Murphy*

_____.*The Hidden Agenda of Sigrid Sugden*

Masters, Anthony. *Bullies Don't Hurt*

Nielsen, Susin. *The Reluctant Journal of Henry K. Larsen*

Palacio, R. J. *Wonder*

Paterson, Katherine. *The Field of Dogs*

Pignat, Caroline. *Egghead*

Preller, James. *Bystander*

Prose, Francine. *Bullyville*

Sachs, Marilyn. *Veronica Ganz*

Shulman, Mark. *Scrawl*

Singer, Nicky. *Feather Boy*

Spinelli, Jerry. *Wringer*

_____. *Stargirl* (Sequel: *Love, Stargirl*)

_____. *Loser*

Stolz, Mary. *The Bully of Barkham Street*

Van Draanen, Wendelin. *Shredderman: Secret Identity*

Wishinsky, Frieda. *So Long, Stinky Queen*

Novels with Innovative Genre Approaches

Verse Novels

Alexander, Kwame. *The Crossover*
Applegate, Katherine. *Home of the Brave*
Burg, Anne E. *All the Broken Pieces*
Cheng, Andrea. *Where the Steps Were*
Cormier, Robert. *Frenchtown Summer*
Creech, Sharon. *Love That Dog*
_____. *Heartbeat.*
_____. *Hate That Cat*
Frost, Helen. *Keesha's House*
_____. *Spinning through the Universe*
Herrick, Steven. *The Simple Gift*
_____. *By the River*
_____. *Naked Bunyip Dancing*
_____. *The Wolf*
Hesse, Karen. *Out of the Dust*
_____. *Witness*
_____. *Aleutian Sparrow*
Hopkins, Ellen. *Tricks*
Koertge, Ron. *The Brimstone Journals*
Lai, Thanhha. *Inside Out and Back Again*
Leavitt, Martine. *My Book of Life by Angel*
Major, Kevin. *Ann and Seamus*
Pinkney, Andrea Davis. *The Red Pencil*
Porter, Pamela. *The Crazy Man*
Rylant, Cynthia. *Boris*
_____. *Ludie's Life*
Smith, Hope Anita. *The Way a Door Closes*
_____. *Keeping the Night Watch*
Wild, Margaret. *Jinx*
Woodson, Jacqueline. *Brown Girl Dreaming*
_____. *Feathers*
_____. *Locomotion* (Sequel: *Peace, Locomotion*)
_____. *After Tupac and D. Foster*

Multi-Genre Novels

Andrews, Jesse. *Me and Earl and the Dying Girl*
Avi. *Nothing but the Truth: A Documentary Novel*
Blos, Joan W. *A Gathering of Days: A New England Girl's Journal, 1830–32*
Carman, Patrick. *Skeleton Creek* (series)
Cushman, Karen. *Catherine Called Birdy*
Durkee, Sarah. *The Fruit Bowl Project*
Gale, Erick Kahn. *The Bully Book*
Hrdlitschka, Shelley. *Sun Signs*
Jocelyn, Marthe. *Mable Riley: A Reliable Record of Humdrum Peril and Romance*
Kinney, Jeff. *Diary of a Wimpy Kid: A Novel in Cartoons*
Mazer, Anne. The Amazing Days of Abby Hayes (series)
Myers, Walter Dean. *Monster*
_____. *Shooter*
Myracle, Lauren. *ttyl* (Sequels: *ttfn; l8r, g8r*)
Rosen, Michael J. *Chaser: A Novel in Emails*
Spearman, Andy. *Barry Boyhound*
Tashjian, Janet. *The Gospel According to Larry*
Townsend, Sue. *The Secret Diary of Adrian Mole, Aged 13¾*
Walters, Eric. *Walking Home*

Graphic Novels

Avi and Brian Floca. *City of Light, City of Dark*
Bell, Cece. *El Deafo*
Bouchard, Hervé, and Janice Nadeau. *Harvey*
Chick, Dixon. *The Hobbit*
L'Engle Madeleine, and Hope Larson. *A Wrinkle in Time*
Myers, Walter Dean, and Christopher Myers. *Autobiography of My Dead Brother*
Reed, Gary. *Frankenstein*

Selznik, Brian. *The Invention of Hugo Cabret*

Satrapi, Marjane. *Persepolis: The Story of a Childhood* (trilogy)

Schade, Susan, and Jon Buller. *Travels of Thelonious* (*The Fog Mound*)

Spiegelman, Art. *Maus: A Survivor's Tale* (Sequel: *Maus II*)

Telgemeire, Raina. *Smile*

Yang, Gene Luen. *American Born Chinese*

Graphic Novel Series

Chantler, Scott. Three Thieves

Crilley, Mark. Akiko

Holm, Jennifer L., and Matthew Holm. Babymouse

Hotta, Yumi. Hikaru No Go

Kibuishi, Kazu. Amulet

Kurumada, Maami. Knights of the Zodiac

Martin, Ann M., and Raina Telgemeire. The Baby-Sitters Club

Ohtaka, Shinobu. Magi

Pilkey, Dav. Captain Underpants

Robinson, James. Leave It to Chance

Scieszka, Jon. The Time Warp Trio

Smith, Jeff. Bone

Stilton, Geronimo. Geronimo Stilton

Takeshi, Hiroyuki. Prince of Tennis

Professional Reading

Allen, Janet. 2000. *Yellow Brick Roads: Shared and Guided Paths to Independent Reading, 4–12.* Portland, ME: Stenhouse.

Atwell, Nancie. 2007. *The Reading Zone: How to Help Kids Become Skilled, Passionate, Habitual, Critical Readers.* New York: Scholastic Teaching Materials.

Beers, Kylene. 2003. *When Kids Can't Read: What Teachers Can Do.* Portsmouth, NH: Heinemann.

Blasingame, James. 2007. *Books That Don't Bore 'Em: Young Adult Books That Speak to This Generation.* New York: Scholastic.

Booth, David. 2002. *Even Hockey Players Read: Boys, Literacy and Learning.* Markham, ON: Pembroke.

_____. 2006. *Reading Doesn't Matter Anymore.* Markham, ON: Pembroke.

_____. 2011. *Caught in the Middle.* Markham, ON: Pembroke.

_____, and Kathleen Gould Lundy. 2007. *In Graphic Detail.* Oakville, ON: Rubicon.

_____, and Larry Swartz. 2010. *Learning to Read with Graphic Power.* Oakville, ON: Rubicon.

_____, Judy Green, and Jack Booth. 2004. *I Want to Read!: Reading, Writing and Really Learning.* Oakville, ON: Rubicon; Toronto: Thomson Nelson.

Carrison, Catherine, and Gisela Ernst-Slavit. 2005. "From Silence to a Whisper to Active Participation: Using Literature Circles with ELL Students." *Reading Horizons,* 46 (2): 93–113.

Clark, Christina. 2013. *Children's and Young People's Reading in 2012: Findings from the 2012 National Literacy Trust's Annual Survey.* London: National Literacy Trust. Retrieved from www.literacytrust.org.uk/ assets/0001/8829/ Young_people_s_reading_2012_-_Final.pdf.

Daniels, Harvey. 2002. *Literature Circles: Voice and Choice in the Student-Centered Classroom.* Markham, ON: Pembroke/Portland, ME: Stenhouse.

Donohue, Lisa. 2008. *Independent Reading: Inside the Box.* Markham, ON: Pembroke.

Foster, Graham. 2012. *Ban the Book Report.* Markham, ON: Pembroke.

Gardiner, Steve. 2005. *Building Student Literacy through Sustained Silent Reading.* Alexandria, VA: ASCD.

Gorman, Michele. 2004. *Going Graphic: Using Graphic Novels to Promote Literacy with Preteens and Teens.* Worthington, OH: Linworth.

Harvey, Stephanie, and Anne Goudvis. 2000. *Strategies That Work: Teaching Comprehension to Enhance Understanding.* Portland, ME: Stenhouse.

Hiebert, Elfrieda, and D. Ray Reutzel, eds. 2010. *Revisiting Silent Reading: New Directions for Teachers and Researchers.* Newark, DE: IRA.

Krashen, Stephen D. 2011. *Free Voluntary Reading*. Santa Barbara, CA: Libraries Unlimited.

Kuta, Katherine Wiesolek, and Susan C. Zernial. 2002. *Novel Ideas for Young Readers*. Englewood, CO: Teacher Ideas Press.

Layne, Steven L. 2015. *In Defense of Read-Aloud: Sustaining Best Practice*. Portland, ME: Stenhouse.

Lewison, Mitzi, Amy Seely Flint, and Katie Van Sluys. 2002. "Taking on Critical Literacy: The Journey of Newcomers and Novices." *Language Arts*, 79 (5): 382–92.

Marshall, Jodi Crum. 2002. *Are They Really Reading? Extending SSR in the Middle Grades*. Portland, ME: Stenhouse.

McGee, Lea M., and Gail E. Tompkins. 1995. "Literature-Based Reading Instruction: What's Guiding the Instruction?" *Language Arts,* 72 (October).

Miller, Donalyn. 2009. *The Book Whisperer: Awakening the Inner Reader in Every Child*. San Francisco, CA: Jossey-Bass.

_____. 2014. *Reading in the Wild: The Book Whisperer's Keys to Cultivating Lifelong Reading Habits*. San Francisco: Jossey-Bass.

Moloney, James. 2000. *Boys and Books: Building a Culture of Reading around Our Boys*. Sydney, AU: ABC Books for the Australian Broadcasting Corporation.

Parr, Judy, and Colleen Maguiness. 2005. "Removing the Silent from SSR: Voluntary Reading as a Social Practice." *Journal of Adolescent and Adult Literacy,* 49: 98–107.

Paul, Kate, and Jennifer Rowsell. 2011. *Literacy and Education: Understanding New Literacies in the Classroom*. London: Sage.

Paterson, Katherine. 1990. *The Spying Heart*. New York: Lodestar.

Pennac, Daniel. 1999. *Better Than Life*. Markham, ON: Pembroke.

Peterson, Shelley Stagg. 2010. *Teaching with Graphic Novels*. Winnipeg, MB: Portage & Main Press.

Peterson, Shelley Stagg, and Larry Swartz. 2008. *Good Books Matter*. Markham, ON: Pembroke.

Sanden, Sherry. 2014. "Out of the Shadow of SSR: Real Teachers' Classroom Independent Reading Practices." *Language Arts* 91 (3): 161–75.

Setterington, Ken, and Deirdre Baker. 2003. *A Guide to Canadian Children's Books in English*. Toronto: McClelland & Stewart.

Sibberson, Frank, and Karen Szymusiak. 2002. *Still Learning to Read: Teaching Students to Read in Grades 3–6*. Portland, ME: Stenhouse.

Silvey, Anita. 2009. *Everything I Need to Know I Learned from a Children's Book*. New York: Roaring Book Press.

Smith, Michael W., & Jeffrey D. Wilhelm. 2002. *Reading Don't Fix No Chevys: Literacy in the Lives of Young Men*. Portsmouth, NH: Heinemann.

Socken, Paul, ed. 2013. *The Edge of the Precipice: Why Read Literature in the Digital Age?* Montreal & Kingston: McGill-Queen's University Press.

Stead, Tony. 2009. *Good Choice! Supporting Independent Reading and Response, K–6*. Portland, ME: Stenhouse.

Swartz, Larry, and David Booth. 2004. *Literacy Techniques: For Building Successful Readers and Writers*. Markham, ON: Pembroke.

Szymusiak, Karen, Frank Sibberson, and Lisa Koch. 2008. *Beyond Leveled Books*. Portland, ME: Stenhouse.

Thompson, Terry. 2008. *Adventures in Graphica: Using Comics and Graphic Novels to Teach Comprehension, 2–6*. Portland, ME: Stenhouse.

Trelease, Jim. 2013. *The Read-Aloud Handbook,* 7th edition. New York: Penguin Books.

Reading Observation Checklist

Name _____

	4 Consistently	3 Often	2 Sometimes	1 Not Yet
Student Reading Behaviors				
Appears to enjoy reading	☐	☐	☐	☐
Tries to finish novels	☐	☐	☐	☐
Can choose novel(s) independently	☐	☐	☐	☐
Concentrates when reading	☐	☐	☐	☐
Focuses on meaning when reading	☐	☐	☐	☐
Student Responses to Novels				
Retells stories	☐	☐	☐	☐
Talks about novels with peers	☐	☐	☐	☐
Writes about novels	☐	☐	☐	☐
Can respond in role	☐	☐	☐	☐
Interprets aspects of the novel through art or other non-print media	☐	☐	☐	☐
Asks thoughtful questions about the novel	☐	☐	☐	☐
Relates novels to personal experiences	☐	☐	☐	☐
Is aware of author's style, language, and vocabulary use	☐	☐	☐	☐
Expresses opinions and demonstrates critical thinking	☐	☐	☐	☐
Chooses response activities independently	☐	☐	☐	☐
Chooses activities that focus on various novel aspects	☐	☐	☐	☐
Is able to promote the novel to others	☐	☐	☐	☐

Comments

_____

_____

_____

Pembroke Publishers © 2015 *"This Is a Great Book!"* by Larry Swartz and Shelley Stagg Peterson ISBN 978-1-55138-308-8

Self-Assessment: Reflecting on Your Novel Reading

1. The novel I recently enjoyed reading the most is _____

   because _____

2. *Place a check mark in one column.*

   I like to respond to the novels by . . .

	Often	Sometimes	Not Yet
writing in a variety of genres (list, diary, letter, script)	☐	☐	☐
writing in a personal response journal	☐	☐	☐
writing in the role of a character	☐	☐	☐
illustrating, designing and constructing (visual arts)	☐	☐	☐
improvising and role-playing (drama)	☐	☐	☐
discussing with a partner or in small groups (talk)	☐	☐	☐
discussing in large groups	☐	☐	☐
researching more about a topic	☐	☐	☐

3. A novel activity I particularly enjoyed was _____ because

   _____.

4. One way that reading the novels has helped me with my reading is _____

   _____.

5. One way that reading the novel(s) has helped me with my writing is _____

   _____.

6. One way that talking about the novel(s) has helped me with my reading is _____

   _____.

7. Things that I find difficult when reading are _____

   Place a check mark beside each point you think can help you with your reading of novels.

   Reading a number of novels in a series _____
   Reading a variety of novel genres _____
   Reading longer books _____
   Working with others who have read the same book that I read _____
   Working with others who have read a different book than I read _____
   Working closely with the teacher to guide me in my reading _____
   Finding a quiet space and time to read _____

8. Describe a goal that you might have for future reading. (You may use the back of this sheet.)

Pembroke Publishers © 2015 *"This Is a Great Book!"* by Larry Swartz and Shelley Stagg Peterson ISBN 978-1-55138-308-8

Reading Observation Checklist

O = Often   S = Sometimes   N = Not yet

Students' names	Dates of observations	Shows enjoyment of reading			Tries to finish novels			Chooses novels independently			Has sustained focus when reading independently			Shows insight into characters/ theme when responding in role			Asks thoughtful questions			Expresses opinions			Demonstrates critical thinking		
		O	S	N	O	S	N	O	S	N	O	S	N	O	S	N	O	S	N	O	S	N	O	S	N

Pembroke Publishers © 2015 *This Is a Great Book!* by Larry Swartz and Shelley Stagg Peterson ISBN 978-1-55138-308-8

Index